Other books by Gordon R. Lewis

Confronting the Cults (Presbyterian and Reformed
Publishing Company)
Decide for Yourself: A Theological Workbook
(InterVarsity Press)

[for those who
are tired of
being told
what to think]

Judge for
Yourself
Gordon R. Lewis

A Workbook on
Contemporary
Challenges to
Christian Faith

InterVarsity Press
Downers Grove, Illinois 60515

InterVarsity Press is the book
publishing division of Inter-Varsity
Christian Fellowship.

The quotation on pages 52-54
is reprinted from Miracles:
Yesterday and Today by
Benjamin B. Warfield, and used
by permission of Wm. B. Eerdmans
Publishing Co., Grand Rapids,
Michigan.

The quotation on pages 101-03
is from the book How Black Is
the Gospel? by Tom Skinner.
Copyright © 1970 by Tom Skinner.
Reprinted as abridged by permission
of J. B. Lippincott Company.

The quotation on pages 103-05
is from Between Two Worlds
by John B. Anderson. Copyright ©
1970 by Zondervan Publishing
House, Grand Rapids, Michigan.
Used by permission.

ISBN: 0-87784-637-5
Library of Congress Catalog Card
Number: 73-81575
Printed in the United States of America

To My Students
in Johnson City, New York, 1951-58
Denver, Colorado, 1958-72
Yeotmal, India, 1973

To the Campus Ministers
who so readily and helpfully
submitted the questions that
introduce each study

And to All Everywhere
who face these crucial questions
with sufficient force to seek
first-hand answers for themselves

Contents

"How . . . shall we ever attain certainty and confidence in our personal and church activity if we do not stand on solid Biblical ground? It is not our heart that determines our course, but God's Word. But who in this day has any proper understanding of the need for scriptural proof? How often we hear innumerable arguments 'from life' and 'from experience' put forward as the basis for most crucial decisions, but the argument of Scripture is missing. And this authority would perhaps point in exactly the opposite direction. It is not surprising, of course, that the person who attempts to cast discredit upon their wisdom should be the one who himself does not seriously read, know, and study the Scriptures. But one who will not learn to handle the Bible for himself is not an evangelical Christian." (Dietrich Bonhoeffer, *Life Together* [New York: Harper, 1954], p. 55)

Preface

Invited to trust Christ as he is presented in the Bible, some college students retort: Who needs Christianity? Isn't traditional morality outmoded? How can a book that old be relevant? At stake in their minds is nothing less than the validity of Christian faith today.

These questions are not merely academic. They often express the struggle of thoughtful people who will not adopt beliefs they do not intend to live by. Students have learned about different cultures and subcultures, philosophies and religions. Their heroes have fallen. They know the pangs of injustice and the experience of suffering. They cringe at the inhumanity of mass technocracies. They are disillusioned by much that goes under the name *Christian.* Their questions come from a distrust of cliches and a search for a reality that will not disappoint them.

If Christian faith is warranted today, these students know they must find that out for themselves. As one put it, "In order for me to have a real relationship with God, I've got to find him by myself." Secondhand religious experience will not do. Little better is secondhand thought about great religious questions.

During a recent semester of teaching in India, I felt with new force the import of such questions. In the drought-ridden State of Maharashtra I saw a portion of one of the world's largest populations—second only to China and growing at a rate of 15 million a year. Most face a frightening struggle for existence. Yet many so treasure spiritual values that they leave what little they do have to go on a pilgrimage in search of peace.

When I learned that less than three per cent of India's masses are in any sense Christian, I joined others in crying out: Is Christ the only way to God? What about those who never heard of Christ or trusted him? Why is there so much suffering in the world? What is the point of occult and miraculous happenings? Why are there so many hypocrites in the Christian church? Does Christianity really work personally and socially in today's world?

According to some recent surveys, these are the questions Christians are most frequently asked on college campuses. In 1971 InterVarsity Press sent a questionnaire to the staff of Inter-Varsity Christian Fellowship. Similarly in 1971 and 1972 I polled the Campus Ambassadors of Conservative Baptist Churches (while meeting with them at their summer Institutes) as well as my students at the Conservative Baptist Theological Seminary. In many different forms (see the beginning of each chapter) these crucial questions kept coming up.

This book has been developed as a guide for those who want to think through these probing issues for themselves. Serious non-Christians are urged to examine Christianity's primary documents to see what the documents actually teach. For purposes of investigation those who do not regard the Bible as an authoritative revelation from God are asked to consider it as the primary source of information on the roots, birth and early growth of Christianity, and on its teaching and way of life. In any research, primary sources take priority over secondary ones. One who has not carefully investigated the biblical materials is ill-equipped to judge the merits of Christianity's claims.

Christians who have agonized over such issues need no further incentive to pursue these studies. Those who have not yet felt them significantly, sooner or later will be brought face to face with them by experience. Sorrow, disillusionment, education, travel, relatives and friends of different persuasions have a way of prompting them. The sheltered may find them uncomfortable, but there is no way successfully to sidestep them.

Furthermore, people often question Christians concerning the faith. Children start asking questions in junior high or high school, and parents, pastors, teachers, counselors, youth ministers, campus workers or church officials are challenged to answer.

Because of misunderstandings, some believers are hesitant to face questions about the validity of their faith. Some think that even to ask such questions is evil. So instead of answering, they attack the person who asks. Or they say that Christianity needs no defense, that the Bible can defend itself. The issue at stake is not the inherent power of God, Christ or the Bible, but the way this power is viewed by young people who during twelve to sixteen years of schooling have heard the Bible's authority questioned and its teachings challenged. To defend is simply to speak in favor of something. Shall these people hear nothing in favor of Christianity? *As far as they are concerned,* does Christianity need no defense?

The Bible itself calls upon Christians to be ready always with an "answer" (1 Pet. 3:15—an apology, a defense as in a court of law). Where are the Lord's servants who are "apt to teach" so that God may deliver those who are ensnared by Satan (2 Tim. 2:24-26)? Let those who "hold fast the faithful word" demonstrate it by "convincing" those who question the Bible's truth and value (Tit. 1:9). In the final analysis, of course, it is the Holy Spirit who does the convincing, but he has chosen to work through human instruments to present his case.

The studies that follow do not treat exhaustively the questions college students ask, but are preliminary investigations of the biblical evidence. Therefore, further readings in secondary sources are listed at the end of each chapter. Because these readings represent each alternative view listed, the reader can enter into the issues more fully. Whatever else one reads, however, the primary biblical materials speak most conclusively.

Work can be done at different levels. Some will want to

examine thoroughly all the questions and passages listed, others may wish to select those of immediate interest to them. Some will have greater ability than others to observe and interpret relevant evidence. Analytical minds will excel in a detailed collection of evidence, synthetical minds will be superior in seeing logical relationships and integrating all lines of evidence in a coherent conclusion. More life-related minds may find it easier to apply the conclusions. The important thing is that each reader works at the level and speed best suited to his particular ability and purpose.

Individuals can work at their own pace. One need not complete a whole study at once, but may take a section at a time. Groups meeting weekly could well spend two, or preferably three, discussions on each chapter. They could divide up the work in Part III of each study, letting a different member or team investigate a certain number of questions. For credit courses in Christian apologetics or related subjects, students could choose two or more studies on which to write papers or prepare reports. Although intended more as a supplementary workbook, this book could serve as the sole text with readings in the footnoted materials (or other readings) also required.

How, then, should you proceed? Here are some hints that may facilitate meaningful research:

1. Write your answers in a large notebook.

2. Have at hand a readable translation of the whole Bible. You may want to compare a second translation on some passages. (Those who can may wish to check the original Hebrew or Greek.)

3. After sharpening the problem in your mind (Step I) and surveying the alternative answers (Step II), begin collecting the relevant data (Step III). In the passages listed, look for explicit or indirect evidence bearing upon the question asked. Each verse can be used for other purposes, too; so do not get sidetracked. Answer the specific question asked, not by copying a listed verse verbatim but by stating the relevant

point in your own words. If you fail to find any connection between verse and question, indicate that. If you think of other passages that help answer the question, add them.

4. Interpret all verses with care, especially those from the Old Testament. They are listed in answer to questions about Christianity because Christians consider them inspired and profitable. However, specific instructions to individials and nations do not directly apply to particular persons and nations now. In those cases, though, a time-transcending principle may be at work which applies to similar situations today. Avoid fanciful spiritualizing of the Old Testament; instead, "principlize" it. (For help on interpreting Scripture, read Bernard Ramm, *Protestant Biblical Interpretation* and Berkeley Mickelsen, *Interpreting the Bible.*)

5. Guard against "prooftexting." When a verse is listed in support of a tenet which contextually it does not teach, the alleged evidence is irrelevant and worthless. The remedy to such misuse of biblical texts, however, is not non-use but responsible use—the scholarly procedure of documenting evidence. Use only those verses that support the precise point at issue.

6. On any given question, summarize all the scriptural data in a statement that is general enough to include all the strands of evidence you found and yet narrow enough not to go beyond what you actually examined.

7. Formulate a conclusion (Step IV), showing that you can do your own research, integrate your findings from throughout the Bible, judge secondary sources by the primary biblical materials (not vice versa), arrive at responsible conclusions, interact significantly with other views (such as those listed in the live options) and state your view with some originality.

8. Show how your conclusion applies to your own life (Step V).

Note that these steps are not repetitious: Each one logically follows the step preceding it. After (1) focusing on the problem and (2) surveying the possible answers, (3) gather and summarize the evidence, (4) integrate all the summations in your conclusion and (5) apply this conclusion to life as you live it.

An earlier volume, *Decide for Yourself: A Theological Workbook* (InterVarsity Press, 1970), applied a similar methodology to questions asked by Christians. Christians have many interesting intramural differences in their understanding of the Bible's teachings, even though they start with the same basic assumptions about God, as he is revealed in the person of Jesus Christ and in the Bible.

The present volume deals with questions frequently asked by non-Christians who do not presuppose the finality of Christ or the authority of Scripture, but are willing to examine the evidence. While the format of the chapters in the two books is similar, the overall assumptions and argument of the books are different. The first is a theological workbook, the second an apologetics workbook. The first treats narrower questions for the purpose of seeing the implications of biblical teaching. The second treats broad questions for the purpose of assessing the validity of biblical presuppositions.

The questions in this book focus primarily upon justifying the claims concerning Christ and the authenticity of life by faith in him. The Christian presupposition concerning the absoluteness of the Bible's teaching remains to be considered. One of the main questions raised in the above-mentioned surveys emphasized the problem of relativism: Isn't all knowledge relative, especially religious knowledge? Rather than include an overly brief and limited treatment of that extensive subject in this book, it has been reserved for one yet to be written. The present book, therefore, does not purport to handle the problems of epistemology and relativism.

For the reader who wants to pursue the literature already available on these questions, I recommend these books: Clark Pinnock's *Biblical Revelation: The Foundation of Christian Theology* (Moody), John W. Wenham's *Christ and the Bible* (InterVarsity), F. F. Bruce's *The New Testament Documents: Are They Reliable?* (InterVarsity), Edward J. Carnell's *Introduction to Christian Apologetics* (Eerdmans), Bernard Ramm's *Protestant Christian Evidences* (Moody) and D. Elton Trueblood's *Philosophy of Religion* (Harper and Row).

I wish to thank students from Inter-Varsity, Campus Ambassadors and Denver Seminary who have contributed realistic questions and stimulated hours of discussion, and to my seminary colleagues who have offered beneficial suggestions and important bibliographical materials.

Gordon R. Lewis
Professor of Systematic Theology and Christian Philosophy
Conservative Baptist Theological Seminary
Denver, Colorado

Is Christ the only way to God?

1

"I'm doing the best I can. Isn't a good moral life enough?"

"My grandmother, who did not accept Christ, was an unselfish hospital worker. Are you telling me she is going to hell?"

"Isn't sincerity enough?"

"God is in everybody, so why this Jesus stuff?"

"Isn't Jesus just another trip?"

"A trip is a trip whether it's on Christ or acid."

"Aren't drugs, yoga, transcendental meditation, Buddha and Mohammed just as good as Jesus?"

"Isn't all religion merely personal insight and experience?"

"Historical claims about a person who lived 2,000 years ago are not enough. I've got to experience God with my whole being, personally."

"Why does salvation have to be through Christ's death? Couldn't God have provided another way?"

"Tolerance is God."

I. The Problem

Whether a person is a skeptic or a believer, if he thinks about Christianity at all he frequently faces the question: "Is faith in Jesus Christ the only way to God?" With so many viewpoints about the way to reach God, a Christian should do more than simply assert his own opinion. Of course, he ought to survey the considered judgments of influential thinkers on the subject. But more importantly, he should rely on the witness of Scripture. Which one of these views fits the greatest amount of relevant Scripture with the fewest difficulties? The present study will try first to survey the major options held today and second to provide a guide to relevant Scripture. The goal is to help people not only to evaluate the options offered in the marketplace of ideas but to come to their own conclusions.

The question of how man can come to God has four basic aspects: (1) the relationship between God's existence and man's existence, (2) man's moral and spiritual position in relation to God, (3) what it means to find God and (4) the way to find God.

II. Live Options

A. Everything in existence constitutes a unity and this all-inclusive unity is divine.[1] Men are part of the divine unity and as such are incarnations of God, as Jesus Christ was. Man's problem is that he thinks he exists as an independent individual apart from God. Man overcomes his suffering as a finite limited being by an immediate experience of union with God. In this mystical union the self is lost in God, time stops, words lose all meaning and one has an inner certainty that he has met ultimate reality.[2] This ecstatic union with

God is the important thing, not how to attain it. Faith in Christ is not the only way. Apart from Christ, men can prepáre for mystical experience by prayer, confession, purification, meditation, disciplined exercise, or viewing the beauties of an illimitable ocean or a majestic mountain range. (Mysticism East and West)

B. According to a second view, a transcendent Lord of the universe is dead. No wise and loving Lord of history is found "up there" or "out there." God is immanent in the world as its ground of being. Man's basic religious problem is that he has withdrawn from the world to seek God privately. By separating himself from the world man has separated himself from God. The way to God is through "incarnate love, a self-giving to the fullness of the world, an immersion in the actuality of time and flesh."[3] Because one meets God in dedicated social action, neither the work of Jesus of Nazareth nor belief in an objective atonement is necessary. (Death of God and secular theologies)

C. Others maintain that we cannot come to God if we confuse him with the world. God in this view is an active, personal being distinct from the universe. Man's basic problem is that he lacks a personal relationship with God. So man's religious objective is not union with God, but communion with him. In coming to God we "turn to the God who has communicated Himself to us, and thereby we withdraw from the world."[4] What God reveals is himself, not information about himself. So belief in the doctrine of God as personal is not as important as the experience of Person-to-person encounter. William Hordern explains, "Christianity is not dedication to a system of rules or of thought, but a dedication to a person. This is unique among the religions of the world."[5] At Denver University's Religion Emphasis Week (1965) Roger Hazelton said that Christianity is "an existential stance before God." He had previously written that the way to God is not through assent to propositions about God and man, Christ and the church, eternity and history. "Christian truth is personal truth, believing trust in response to God's gracious overture in Christ."[6] (Neo-Orthodoxy)

D. Without information about God, mystical experiences, personal encounters or an existential stance may relate a person to an idol rather than to God. The way to the living God who is there is found with the help of a good "map"—true information about him. Divinely revealed truth informs us that God is a tri-personal, active Being, distinct from the universe. Man's basic religious problem is not only a lack of personal relationship with God but also moral guilt and inner depravity. Unable to change our own creature-centered nature, justify ourselves or return to God's fellowship, we face death. But God so loved the world that he sent his eternal Son to die our death and rise again. Christ's atonement alone meets man's three basic needs by providing (1) liberation from his selfish propensity, (2) the satisfaction of justice and (3) reconciliation to personal fellowship with God.

These provisions become ours, however, only through our trust in the crucified and risen Christ. Apart from faith in Christ as Savior and Lord we remain under the just sentence of death, unregenerate and at enmity with God. Faith can come only by hearing the gospel. Christianity is life founded upon doctrine.[7] Christ came in the flesh, died for our sins and rose again the third day according to the Scriptures. The Christian movement at its inception was not just a way of life in the modern sense, but a way of life founded upon this message.[8] All who receive this message and trust the real Christ are forgiven all their sin, justified before divine law, given a new nature and restored to personal fellowship with God. (Orthodoxy)

III. Debated Issues and Biblical Data

A. The relationship between God's existence and man's existence

1. Is God the unity of all that exists, or is he an active, personal being whose life, thought, will and power are indepen-

dent of his creation in eternal changelessness?

Ps. 90:1-2	Ps. 115:3	Jn. 5:26
Ps. 102:25-27	Dan. 4:35	Rom. 11:33-34

2. When Paul addressed the Stoic variety of pantheism, what affirmations and negations did he make regarding God and his relations to the world?

Acts 17:24-29

3. Is it possible to make meaningful statements about God (that is, statements which communicate something about who God is), or can a person only experience him?

Ex. 3:13-15	Ps. 19:7-10	Mt. 24:35
Ex. 34:5-8	Ps. 119:13-18	Acts 26:12-18

4. Is God incarnate in every person, in the same way he is in Christ, or is Jesus Christ the completely unique Son of God?

Mt. 23:8-10	Jn. 5:33-47	Phil. 2:5-11
Jn. 1:1, 14, 18	Jn. 6:38-51	Heb. 1:1-8
Jn. 3:27-36	Jn. 8:23-30, 58	

5. What does a person need to believe about God in order to come to him?

Heb. 11:6

6. Summarize this section by discussing the question: God is in everybody, so why this Jesus stuff?

B. Man's moral and spiritual problem in relation to God

1. Is man's basic religious problem that he is a finite individual distinct from God, or can a finite person be in a right relationship with God?

Gen. 1:27-31	Rev. 21:3-4	Rev. 22:3-5

2. If people are dependent upon God for life and breath, does it follow that they are right with God morally and spiritually?

Acts 17:30-31	Rom. 1:21-23	Rom. 3:10-18, 23

3. Is man's problem that he lacks personal rapport with God?

Rom. 5:10	Eph. 4:18	Col. 1:21
Eph. 2:12, 19		

4. How righteous does man need to be to please God? Does man's religious problem involve legal guilt and condemnation before the bar of divine justice?

Jn. 3:18	Rom. 2:12-16	Rom. 3:19-20
Rom. 1:18, 20	Rom. 3:9-10	Rom. 5:16, 18

5. Is fallen man's problem also the depravity of his own heart, which is bent toward sinning?

Gen. 6:5	Jer. 17:9	Eph. 2:3
Ps. 51:5	Mt. 15:18-19	Eph. 4:18
Is. 48:8	Jn. 3:6	Jas. 4:1-2
Is. 64:6	Rom. 7:18-19	

6. What is the eventual result of sin?

Prov. 14:12	Rom. 5:12	Jas. 1:15
Ezek. 18:20	Rom. 6:23	

7. Summarize this section by discussing whether a person's sincerity or good moral life is enough to enable him to meet God.

C. What Jesus Christ did to overcome man's moral and spiritual difficulties

1. After man sinned, could God have gone back on his word "the soul that sins shall die," even though keeping his word might seem to mean the defeat of his purpose for creating man in his image?

2 Tim. 2:13	Tit. 1:2

2. Why didn't God destroy man after man sinned?

Ps. 136:23	Eph. 1:5	1 Jn. 4:8-10
1 Cor. 13:7		

3. Why did the eternal Word of God, who created all things, become a man and live on earth?

Heb. 2:9-18

4. How did Jesus' death provide deliverance from bondage to sin?

Mt. 20:28	Rom. 8:2-4	Eph. 1:7
Jn. 8:34-36	Gal. 4:4-5	Tit. 2:14

5. How does Jesus' death enable God to remain just and yet not permit sinners who believe in him to suffer the death

they deserve?

Is. 53:6	2 Cor. 5:21	1 Jn. 2:2
Rom. 3:25-26	1 Pet. 3:18	1 Jn. 4:10

6. How does Christ's death make possible man's restoration to personal fellowship with God?

Rom. 5:10-11	Eph. 2:12-16	Col. 1:20-22
2 Cor. 5:18-20		

7. By obeying God's law, can sinful people attain spiritual life and righteousness apart from Christ?

Gal. 3:10-11, 21-24

8. Is there anyone other than Christ who is (1) not corrupted by sin, (2) able to recreate man in God's image, (3) worthy to die for all men and (4) able to identify fully with both God and man as a mediator?

Jn. 14:6	Acts 4:12	1 Tim. 2:5-6

9. Summarize this section by answering these questions: Why does salvation have to be through Christ's death? Couldn't God have provided another way?

D. What it means to find God through Christ

1. What does it mean to come to God by faith in Christ?

Jn. 1:12	Jn. 7:38-39	Rom. 5:1
Jn. 3:16, 18	Acts 10:43	2 Cor. 5:17-21
Jn. 5:24	Acts 16:31	1 Jn. 1:3
Jn. 6:40	Rom. 4:5	

2. Does a Christian's experience of God make historical events (in time and space) unimportant?

2 Pet. 1:16-18	1 Jn. 1:1-3

3. In a Christian's experience of God do words lose all meaning?

Jn. 6:63, 68	Jn. 20:21	Acts 9:1-22
Jn. 14:23-26	Acts 2:36, 41-42	2 Jn. 9
Jn. 15:7		

4. In experiencing God does a Christian lose his distinct individuality in the being of God, or does he come into a personal fellowship with God?

Acts 9:1-22	Gal. 2:20	1 Pet. 4:2

Rom. 6:11   1 Thess. 5:10   1 Jn. 1:3
2 Cor. 5:15

5. Is certainty of one's acceptance with God based on the psychological phenomenon of certitude itself or on God-given promises illumined by the Holy Spirit?

Rom. 8:8-17   Gal. 4:6-7   2 Thess. 2:13-17
2 Cor. 4:3-18   1 Thess. 2:13   1 Jn. 5:10-13

6. Summarize this section by discussing the questions, Isn't Jesus just another trip? Isn't all religion merely personal insight and experience?

E. The way to God: trusting the Christ of the gospel

1. Must a person stop trying to get to God in other ways and trust Christ alone?

Lk. 16:13   Acts 2:38   Acts 20:21
Lk. 24:47   Acts 3:19   2 Cor. 7:10
Jn. 14:6   Acts 4:12   1 Thess. 1:9

2. Are there "counterfeit Christs" who seek people's allegiance?

Mt. 24:23-24   Mk. 13:21-22   1 Jn. 2:18-19, 22-23

3. How can one know that his confidence is placed in the real Christ?

1 Jn. 4:1-3   2 Jn. 9

4. What teachings (doctrines) lead a person to the Christ who saves?

Jn. 1:1, 12, 14   Jn. 20:31   Rom. 10:9-10
Jn. 8:23-24, 58   Rom. 3:24-25

5. How does the apostle Paul sum up the heart of the message (the gospel) he presented to pre-Christians?

1 Cor. 15:1-4

6. Is there more than one gospel?

Gal. 1:8-9

7. Did people who lived before the time of Christ come to God without believing in the coming Christ, or did they have faith in the promised descendant of Eve, Abraham and David who would be born of a virgin in Bethlehem and bring the blessing of salvation to the world?

Gen. 3:15	Is. 7:14	Gal. 3:8, 16
Gen. 12:3	Mic. 5:2	Heb. 11:10, 13, 26
Gen. 15:4-6	Rom. 4:3, 6, 13	1 Pet. 1:10-12
2 Sam. 7:12-13	Rom. 4:20-25	

8. Can a person who has not heard about the true Christ through the gospel have an implicit faith in Christ?

Acts 10:1-3, 22, 34-43 Rom. 10:13-18[9] Jn. 10:16
Rom. 2:7

9. Summarize this section by answering the question: What difference does it make what one believes about Jesus, so long as he is sincere?

IV. Conclusion

Formulate your answer to the question "Is faith in Christ the only way to God?" by pulling together your summaries of the preceding sections, evaluating the live options (II) with which you differ and interacting with any reading you have done in the sources listed in the notes below.[10]

V. Relevance

A. Experientially, what have you found it means to come to God through faith in Christ?

B. If you have come to God by faith in Christ, what are you doing to help pre-Christians in your own locality and around the world come to the Savior?

Notes

1 Alasdair MacIntyre, "Pantheism," *The Encyclopedia of Philosophy,* ed. Paul Edwards (New York: The Macmillan Company and the Free Press, 1967), VI, p. 34.

2 Walter T. Stace, *Mysticism and Philosophy* (Philadelphia and New York: J. B. Lippincott, 1960), pp. 277-306; William Braden, *The Private Sea: LSD and the Search for God* (Chicago: Quadrangle Books, 1967), pp. 15-45.

3 Thomas J. Altizer, *The Gospel of Christian Atheism* (Philadelphia: The Westminster Press, 1967), p. 156.

4 Emil Brunner, *The Christian Doctrine of the Church, Faith and Consummation* (Philadelphia: The Westminster Press, 1960), p. 324.

5 William Hordern, *A Layman's Guide to Protestant Theology* (New York: The Macmillan Company, 1960), p. 190.

6 Roger Hazelton, *New Accents in Contemporary Theology* (New York: Harper and Brothers, 1960), p. 137.

7 J. Gresham Machen, *What Is Christianity?* (Grand Rapids: Wm. B. Eerdmans, 1951), p. 22.

8 J. Gresham Machen, *Christianity and Liberalism* (Grand Rapids: Wm. B. Eerdmans, 1946), p. 21. Cf. the older classics, St. Athanasius, *De Incarnatione Verbi Dei (The Incarnation of the Word of God),* trans. by a Religious of C.S.M.V. (New York: The Macmillan Company, 1946), pp. 1-96; St. Anselm, *Cur Deus Homo (Why God Became a Man),* trans. Sidney Norton Deane (La Salle, Ill.: The Open Court, 1951), pp. 171-288.

9 If you have studied Gordon Lewis, *Decide for Yourself* (Downers Grove, Ill.: Inter-Varsity Press, 1970), chapter one, consider your findings on the content universally revealed (gospel?) and the end result of that revelation (salvation?).

10 Compare your conclusion here to that of *Decide for Yourself,* study 16.

What about those who have never heard of Christ or trusted him?

2

"What about people who have never heard the good news of Jesus Christ?"

"Are they damned simply because of their location?"

"Is there no hope for the sincere followers of other religions?"

"What about the devotees of Eastern mysticism?"

"In this enlightened age, surely you don't consider any people heathen!"

I. The Problem

People aware of Christ's unique provision for redemption are properly concerned for those who have not heard or accepted it. But emotionally laden questions are not settled simply by the intensity of our convictions. We may be merely sentimental, or cold and uncaring. The genuine inquirer seeks to control his emotions and examine the available evidence. The final court of appeal is not the prevailing opinion at a given time, but divine revelation. An authentic inquiry calls for a willingness to follow the biblical evidence wherever it leads. The problem, then, is determining what the Bible actually teaches about those who have not heard the gospel or trusted Christ. Not all interpreters of Scripture are agreed on this controversial issue.

II. Live Options

A. According to some, no unbelievers will ultimately be lost. Sooner or later, all will be reconciled to God through Christ. Christ died for all men of all times and places. Divine grace and power will triumph over the most obdurate. God is a pedagogue who has no incorrigible students. Believers could not enjoy their salvation so long as one person remained in unbelief.[1] (Universalists)

B. Others maintain that only those unbelievers who live up to the way of morality or religion they know will be accepted by God. Whatever his beliefs, if a man does the best he can with what he does know, God's love will embrace him. The experience of salvation does not require any doctrinal beliefs but is an experience of religious peace and brotherly love. God's grace overflows the boundaries of orthodox theology and is not the monopoly of the Christian community.

In any religion people may experience salvation.[2] (World Religionists)

C. Others hold out hope for those who have not heard of Christ, not on the basis of works but of repentance. The Bible denies the possibility of any person earning salvation by trying to be good or religious. But everyone is divinely enabled to repent of his sin. If a person "realizes something of his sin or need and throws himself upon the mercy of God with a sincerity that shows itself in his life," he will find mercy because of the cross. The essential elements of salvation, then, do not include a hearing of the gospel, but "a God-given sense of sin or need, and a self-abandonment to God's mercy."[3] (Some Evangelicals)

D. Every man is responsible to live up to (1) the truth about God that may be known in nature and the truth about morality that may be known in his own heart, (2) the standards of Moses' law if he has lived under it and (3) the message of the gospel if he has heard it. No man is all that he ought to be, and consequently all men are under judgment for their failure to practice the truth they do know. The hope of salvation for any man is not in self-justification but in justification by the sheer grace of God through faith in his just provision. Instances of alleged penitents who never hear of Christ need to be checked out further. Those recorded in Scripture and by many missionaries disclose a subsequent opportunity to trust the Savior followed by a glad acceptance of him. Some special means of applying the benefits of Christ's atonement to infants who die and grown people who are not morally responsible may be inferred from biblical principles. All accountable persons, however, inexcusably fall short of moral and spiritual norms and can justly be declared righteous only through faith in the gospel.[4] (Some Evangelicals)

III. Debated Issues and Biblical Data
A. Sincere people in non-Christian religions
Judaism has more in common with Christianity than do

any of the world's religions. Rooted in the Old Testament and the traditions of rabbinical scholarship, Judaism abhors idolatry, maintains strict monotheism, teaches high ethical standards and observes significant ceremonies. In New Testament times the Pharisees were among the most sincere Jews. Paul was one of the most zealous of the Pharisees.

1. Did Paul regard sincere followers of Judaism lost? Why?

Rom. 10:1-3

2. What is the difference between what Christianity and Judaism teach about righteousness?

Rom. 1:17   Rom. 4:3-6, 9-13, 22   Gal. 2:14—3:29
Rom. 3:21-26   Rom. 5:17, 21

3. Can a religion (like that of the Pharisees) promote many good things and yet miss more important ones?

Mt. 23:23   Lk. 11:42

4. Does faith in Christ destroy the law of Moses or fulfill it?[5]

Mt. 5:17-18   Rom. 8:3-4   Rom. 13:8-10
Rom. 7:12

5. Did Paul try to persuade Jews to become Christians?

Acts 13:5, 14, 42-44   Acts 17:1-3   Acts 19:8-9
Acts 14:1   Acts 18:4, 19

The ancient Stoics were religious philosophers concerned about attaining the good life. God was the unchanging law of change, determining what everything would be and do. Men were considered a brotherhood in the image of God because they were not merely passive, but active. Like many sincere people today, the Stoics thought of God as the immanent Father of all men and of all men as brothers. Many of those who listened to Paul in Athens (Acts 17:16-34) would have been influenced by Stoicism.

6. As Paul addressed the religious people at Athens, the university center of the Greek world, did he find anything in their religious ideas or practices with which he could agree?

Acts 17:22-28

7. Did Paul consider it imperative to preach the gospel to the cultured Athenians?
Acts 17:29-34

8. What is Paul's reaction to the Greeks at Lystra? How did Paul contrast his message with their perception?
Acts 14:15-17

9. Summarize this section and show how your findings apply to Eastern mysticism and other contemporary religions.

B. Divine judgment

1. Are all people God's people morally and spiritually?

Mt. 7:13-29	Mt. 13:36-43	Mt. 25:41-46
Mt. 10:32-39	Mt. 15:7-9	Jn. 1:10-13

2. How many persons have been under divine condemnation?

Jn. 3:18, 36	Rom. 3:10-23	Rom. 5:16-18

3. Upon what grounds is God's judgment pronounced and its penalty received?

Ps. 19:1-6	Acts 17:26-29	Rom. 2:5, 12, 14
Jn. 3:17-18, 36	Rom. 1:18-22	Rom. 2:17—3:10
Acts 14:16-17		

4. Is a person justified before God by doing the best he can, by feeling sorry he has not done as well as he should or by what?

Rom. 2:6-10	Rom. 4:24-25	Gal. 2:16
Rom. 3:21-28	Rom. 5:9, 16	Jas. 2:20-26

5. Are those who never heard of Christ condemned on the basis of not believing in Christ, or do they remain under condemnation on other bases?
Jn. 3:17-18, 36
Compare passages in B3.

6. Summarize this section by evaluating this statement of G. Campbell Morgan: "We may speak of degrees of light [truth] and indeed we must so speak. To imagine that vast multitudes of the heathen [unbelievers] are to be consigned to everlasting punishment because they have not

obeyed the gospel which we have never preached to them, is blasphemy of the worst kind. The measure of heathen responsibility is the measure of heathen light. Light creates responsibility. Sin is disobedience to light."

C. The unbeliever's destiny

1. Is much of the unbeliever's punishment the inevitable result of his chosen way of life?

Ps. 37:15   Prov. 26—27   Gal. 6:7-8
Prov. 5:22   Mt. 7:2

2. Is a person's eternal destiny determined at his death, or is there an opportunity for choice after death?

Heb. 9:27   1 Pet. 3:18-20

3. Is the future of those who persist in unbelief restorative so that, like a purgatory, it eventually saves them, or are the consequences of unbelief eternal?[6]

Mt. 12:31-32   Mk. 9:43-48   2 Cor. 5:19
Mt. 25:31-46   Lk. 3:17   1 Tim. 2:4
Mk. 3:29-30   Jn. 3:36

4. Is the unbeliever's punishment retributive (that is, not for the purpose of reformation but for vindication of justice)?[7]

2 Pet. 3:7   Rev. 20:10-15

5. Are there varying degrees of punishment according to the degree of opportunity rejected?

Mt. 11:21-24   Lk. 12:47-48   Heb. 2:2-3

6. Are there any principles illustrated in Scripture that indicate the possibility of a special application of Christ's atonement for infants who were never individually accountable?

Deut. 1:39   Mt. 18:3-14   Mt. 19:14
Jn. 4:11

7. Summarize this section and then interact with this statement of theologian Charles Hodge: "The sufferings of the finally impenitent, according to the Scriptures arise: (1) From the loss of all earthly good. (2) From exclusion from the presence and favor of God. (3) From utter reprobation, or the final withdrawal of the Holy Spirit. (4) From the conse-

quent unrestrained dominion of sin and sinful passions. (5) From the operations of conscience. (6) From despair. (7) From their evil associates. (8) From their external circumstances ... (9) From their perpetuity."

D. The trustworthiness of God

1. What does it mean for God to be "just"? (Check dictionary.) Is God unjust in condemning those who do not accept his redemptive provision? On the other hand, would God be just if he did not judge sinners?

Deut. 25:16	Ps. 111:3	Col. 3:25
2 Chron. 19:7	Ps. 145:17	1 Pet. 1:17
Ps. 19:9	Rom. 3:5-6	1 Jn. 3:4

2. If God offers salvation to many men, is it *necessary* that he offer salvation to all men? If divine grace is totally undeserved favor freely given, can God be under obligation to give it to all?

Rom. 3:24	Eph. 1:5-8	Eph. 2:8
Rom. 9:14-24		

3. No man may justly be penalized for anything he does not deserve. Does it follow that no one can justly receive undeserved good that others do not receive?

Mt. 20:1-16

4. While there may be much we cannot now understand about the destiny of unbelievers, have we reason to believe that God will not permit injustice to any?

Gen. 18:25	Lam. 3:22-23	Rom. 5:8
Num. 23:19	Jn. 3:16	Rom. 8:32
Josh. 23:14	Rom. 2:5, 16	2 Tim. 4:8

5. Does God take any pleasure in the punishment of the finally unbelieving?

Ezek. 18:23, 32	2 Pet. 3:9	1 Tim. 2:4

6. Summarize this section by evaluating the charge that God is uncaring and unjust if all men are not saved.

IV. Conclusion

Formulate your answer to the question "What about those

who never heard of Christ or trusted him?" by pulling together your summaries of the preceding sections, evaluating the live options (II) with which you differ and interacting with any reading you have done in the sources listed in the notes below.[8]

V. Relevance
A. When you face God, the issue will not be others, but yourself. On what basis do you expect to be accepted by a holy God?

B. Do the people you meet daily have an adequate basis for acceptance with God?

Notes

[1] Nels Ferre, *Christ and the Christian* (New York: Harper and Brothers, 1958), p. 248; *Evil and the Christian Faith* (New York: Harper and Brothers, 1947), p. 117f.

[2] Woodbridge O. Johnson, "Non-Christian Salvation," *The Journal of Bible and Religion*, 31 (July 1963), 216-24; Vergilius Ferm, ed., *Twentieth Century Religion* (New York: The Philosophical Library, 1948), pp. v-xv.

[3] J. N. D. Anderson, *Christianity and Comparative Religion* (Downers Grove, Ill.: InterVarsity Press, 1970), pp. 102, 105. See also A. H. Strong, *Systematic Theology* (Philadelphia: Judson Press), pp. 843-44; W. G. T. Shedd, *Dogmatic Theology* (Grand Rapids: Zondervan, n.d.), II, pp. 704-12.

[4] Charles Hodge, *Systematic Theology* (Grand Rapids: Wm. B. Eerdmans, 1946), II, pp. 646-48. Cf. Robert E. Speer, *The Finality of Jesus Christ* (Westwood, N.J.: Fleming H. Revell, n.d.).

[5] John E. Meeter, ed., *Selected Shorter Writings of Benjamin B. Warfield* (Nutley, N.J.: Presbyterian and Reformed, 1970), pp. 27, 45. Warfield saw that the relationship between general revelation and special revelation "is not one of contrast and opposition, but rather one of supplement and completion" (p. 27). So he asserts, "All religion and all the morality which has ever been in the world is of God. Whether natural or revealed, it is he who has given it; and it is he alone who has maintained it, yea, and will maintain it; enlarged and enriched to meet sinful man's clamant needs and renewed man's deeper desires. Both religion and morality are rooted in God, live in God, and in all the states of their development, and phases of their manifestation alike reflect man's essential relations to God—relations of dependence and obligation."

[6] Henry Nutcombe Oxenham, *Catholic Eschatology* (London: Basil Montagn Pickering, 1876), p. 45: "Once admit, what is evident, that the created will has the power of rebelling against its Maker, and there is absolutely no ground in reason for assuming that the rebellion, and therefore the chastisement, must sooner or later necessarily have an end. Revelation might have told us so, but it has not. Reason, as far as it throws any light on the question, points the other way." M. Randlers, *Forever* (London: Wesleyan Conference Office, 1878), p. 61: "Why have we not one word from the lips of the Great Teacher to indicate the possibility, if not the certainty of escape or deliverance? If there was a door of hope, how unlike the Loving Lamb to conceal it!"

[7] Immanuel Kant, *Praktische Vernuft*, p. 151, cited by William G. T. Shedd, *The Doctrine of Endless Punishment* (New York: Charles Scribner's Sons, 1886), pp. 122-23: "The notion of ill desert and punishableness is necessarily implied in the idea of voluntary transgression; and the idea of punishment excludes that of happiness in all its forms. For though he who inflicts punishment may, it is true, also have a benevolent purpose to produce by the punishment some good effect upon the criminal, yet the punishment must be justified first of all, as pure and simple requital and retribution: that is, as a kind of suffering that is demanded by the law without any reference to its prospective beneficial consequences; so that even if no moral improvement and no personal advantage should subsequently accrue to the criminal, he must acknowledge that justice has been done to him, and that his experience is exactly conformed to his conduct. In every instance of punishment, properly so called, justice is the first thing, and constitutes the essence of it."

A benevolent purpose and a happy effect, it is true, may be conjoined with punishment, but the criminal cannot claim this as his due, and he has no right to reckon upon it. All that he deserves is punishment, and this is all that he can expect from the law that he has transgressed."
[8] Compare this with your conclusion to study 1 in *Decide for Yourself.*

Why is there so much suffering in the world?

3

"Why does God allow ghettos and racism?"

"Why is there sickness, disease and death?"

"Why is there any pain at all?"

"How can a good God condone war?"

"How can God say 'Thou shalt not kill' and then command Israel to annihilate Canaanite cities?"

"If God is a God of love, how could he instruct his selected people to behave in such a brutal way?"

"Did God create evil?"

"If God made everything, then he must have made sin and evil. So how could a God who is good create evil? Or how could he put the punishment of sin upon all men simply because of one man's mistakes?"

"Why did God create man and this whole world when he knew what would happen anyway?"

"Are Christians to expect suffering in their lives, or is the abundant life one of continual joy and happiness?"

"Why doesn't God do something about the tragic evils in the world?"

I. The Problem

As the daily news reminds all of us, we are caught up in a world of injustice and tragedy. At times, accidents and illnesses, prejudice and misrepresentation hurt our closest friends. We cry out, Why? Why must such things happen? Why did God let this happen to me?

Concern about the problem of evil is not necessarily a sign of unbelief. Such concern may indicate a quest for a realistic, costly faith. Cheap faith either does not see the problem or sees it but does not feel it. Hardness of heart is the father of cheap faith.[1]

Who can see starving little children in a ghetto or terminal patients in a hospital without wondering why God allows such frightful things to happen? Is he unable or unwilling to wipe out the enormity of evil that human beings suffer?

Many would like to find springs of courage, counsel and action to alleviate the suffering of people while bypassing the hard work of thinking through the difficult issues of the nature of evil, its origin and its relation to divine sovereignty. However, if our programs are built upon a superficial diagnosis of the problem, its ultimate cause and relation to God, eventually we will be further disappointed. While alleviating symptoms is important, even more important is treating real causes. Unless the power of positive thinking is rooted in reality, it may be little more than the power of wishful thinking.

This study asks the reader to face these problems squarely, consider the alternative answers, examine the Scripture, formulate a conclusion and apply the principles discovered to a concrete instance of human tragedy.

II. Live Options

A. According to Vedanta teachings in Hinduism, the phenomenal world with all its evils is illusion (*maya*). There are not many kinds of things, but in reality only one. The one ultimate reality is Brahman. Appearances to the contrary, reality is good.[2] In the Western world, Christian Science has also maintained that reality is one, divine and good, and that evil is illusory. There are not two ultimate realities, but one. All is divine Mind and his idea. "The only reality of sin, sickness, or death is the awful fact that unrealities seem real to human, erring belief, until God strips off their disguise. . . . We learn in Christian Science that all inharmony of mortal mind or body is illusion."[3]

B. From another extreme, the reality and pervasiveness of evil are explained by a Source as ultimate and eternal as God. Good and evil, according to Zoroastrianism, are utterly irreconcilable and opposed to each other. There can be no peace or harmony between them. Their duality can be overcome only by one defeating the other. Angra Mainyu (or Ahriman), the eternal evil deity, and Ahura Mazda (or Ormuzd), the eternal good deity, seek men to fight on their side. Zoroaster summoned men to do battle for good against evil.[4] Another variety of dualism appeared in Plato's thought. He suggested that a good but limited deity was only partially able to control the independent realm of chaotic and intractable matter. This raw material which the Maker of the world utilized is the source of evil. Only good can be attributed to God. More recently, John Stuart Mill held that God was limited by the substances and forces of the universe. God's creative skill, wonderful as it is, is not sufficient to accomplish his purposes more completely.[5] The problem of evil has also caused Edgar S. Brightman and Peter Bertocci to defend the view that God is finite.

C. All suffering, according to a popular view, is a divine judgment upon some specific sin. When tragedy strikes, people often ask, "What did I do to deserve this?" For example, Job's friends suggested that he lost his health, family and possessions because of a sin he committed. Some promoters of divine healing adopt this viewpoint, insisting that it is never God's will for any Christian to suffer and that every illness is a judgment upon the victim's sin.[6]

D. Some people believe that suffering is never judgmental but is instrumental in bringing about good, in an evolutionary development of human character. John Hick suggests that the story of Adam's Fall is mythological. Man never existed in a state of pre-Fall perfection nor descended to a state of depravity. The story of the Fall is an analysis of man's present condition of estrangement from God, not an account of how he came to this state. As man emerged from lower forms of life, he was endowed with only dim and rudimentary conceptions of his Maker. Although God made man with this original lack of knowledge of him, men are responsible for their personal choices and actions. The God who made man imperfect but perfectible has entered life in Christ to bring about man's reconciliation. This world of mingled good and evil is a divinely appointed environment for man's development toward the perfection that represents the fulfillment of God's good purpose for him. Sin prepares the way for grace; grace does not occur to repair the damage of sin. Ultimately God alone is sovereign, and evil can exist only by his permission. Thus God has willed to create a universe in which it is better for him to permit sin and evil than not to permit them. So evil is instrumental to divine purposes. These purposes will be fully realized in the triumph over all evil in the last days. The end to which God is leading all men (universalism) is a good so great it will justify all the failures and suffering and sorrow that will have been endured on the way.[7]

E. All things were created by God out of nothing and are sustained according to the divine plan. God alone is eternal; he is not limited by an eternal evil being nor by eternal, intractable matter. Everything that God created was very good.

God made men and angels with the power of free will. Not even omnipotence itself could create a moral being without the possibility of disobedience as well as obedience. Omnipotence can do everything it chooses in the way it chooses, but it cannot do contradictory nothings like creating a will which cannot will. Sin originated with the culpable volition of free creatures. Although God is the final cause of everything that is, creatures, not God, were the efficient, blameworthy causes of sin. God permitted but did not determine the misuse of the human will. The sin of man consisted not in choosing a positive evil (for there is no positive evil to choose), but in turning away from the higher good (God) to a lower good (the creature). God remains sovereign over sin and sinful creatures, restraining moral evil and overruling it. God judges sin at Calvary but suffers with sinners empathically and vicariously through the sacrifice of Christ at Calvary. The resurrected Lord has won the decisive battle with evil and secured the ultimate triumph of good over evil.

Some suffering in the world is empathic and vicarious. Some serves God's purpose as a warning to prevent greater evil; some is disciplinary for training in Christlikeness and for a witness to one's allegiance to God. Natural evils serve a number of different purposes in God's plan. Ultimately natural evils are the result of the entrance of moral evil into the world through man's Fall. Only some natural disasters, however, may be traced to judgment upon the sins of men or nations. When God's purposes for history are completed, he will create a new heaven and earth without sin or sorrow, making all present trials seem insignificant by comparison.[8]

III. Debated Issues and Biblical Data
A. The nature of evil

1. Is there an objective difference between good and evil, right and wrong, justice and injustice?

Is. 5:20   Mic. 3:1-2   Rom. 12:9, 21

Amos 5:14-15   Mal. 2:17

2. What attitudes and acts may be listed as specific examples of evil among morally responsible human beings? (You may want to list instances of good attitudes and acts by way of contrast.)

Gal. 5:19-26   Col. 3:5-17   Tit. 3:3-5
Eph. 4:17—5:20

3. Formulate a general statement about how God views all instances of moral evil. (You may also want to formulate a definition of how God sees the good.)

Ex. 34:6-7   Is. 59:2   Rom. 1:18
Ps. 5:4   Ezek. 18:23-32   1 Jn. 1:5-10
Ps. 101:7-8   Mic. 6:6-8

4. Are there natural evils for which man is not morally responsible?

Mt. 24:7   Acts 16:26   Rev. 16:18
Mt. 27:54   Rev. 11:13

5. Is all evil an illusion of the human, mortal mind?

Gen. 2:2-5   Judg. 2:10-15   Mt. 23:13-36
Gen. 6:5-7   Is. 1:4-31   Rom. 1:18-32

6. Is the absence of good, the omission of proper choices and actions an evil?

Is. 26:18   Mt. 25:45   1 Cor. 13:2
Mt. 23:3, 23   Rom. 7:19   Jas. 4:17

7. Summarize this section by answering the question, What is evil?

B. The origin of evil

1. Did sin originate with an evil being who exists eternally? Is there an eternal dualism of good and evil beings?

Deut. 4:35   Lk. 11:15-19   2 Pet. 2:4
Ps. 148:2, 5   Eph. 2:2   1 Jn. 3:8-9
Is. 45:5   Col. 1:16   Jude 6
Mt. 3:1-11   1 Tim. 3:6   Rev. 12:7-12
Lk. 10:17-19   1 Tim. 6:16

2. Does evil come from matter, which is an eternal entity resisting the power and purpose of God? Is man's body, for

example, the source of his sin?

Gen. 1:1-10, 31   1 Tim. 4:1-5   Heb. 11:3
Jn. 1:3

3. Is the account of Adam and Eve's Fall in Eden a mythological story portraying man's present experience of falling into sin, or does it literally inform us of sin's origin at the beginning of the human race?

Gen. 3:1-24   1 Cor. 15:21-22   2 Cor. 11:3
Mt. 19:4   1 Cor. 15:45, 47   1 Tim. 2:13-14

4. Did man's sin arise from non-moral influences of an animal existence from which he is still evolving, or did sin originate in the misuse of man's will?

Gen. 1:21, 26-27   Rom. 5:12-18   1 Tim. 2:13-14
Gen. 3:1-24   2 Cor. 11:3

5. From what source did man's temptation to sin come?

Gen. 3:1-5, 13-15   2 Cor. 11:3   Rev. 12:9
Mt. 13:24-30, 36-39   1 Jn. 3:8

6. Summarize this section by answering the question, Where did evil come from?[9]

C. Divine sovereignty and the origin of evil

1. While the blameworthy or effecting cause of moral evil was men and angels (who produced it by their activity), was God the final cause of evil (that is, did he design the purpose or goal of the effecting causes)? In other words, does evil arise by chance as an independent and uncontrollable principle, or does it occur by divine will?

Ps. 76:1-12   Is. 46:8-11   Eph. 1:11

2. Does God will evil with pleasure in the same sense that he wills good? May one distinguish God's permissive will (done with displeasure) from his positive will (done with pleasure)?

Ps. 81:11-13   Acts 14:16   Phil. 2:13
Is. 14:24, 27   Rom. 1:24-28

3. Did God tempt Adam and Eve to do evil?

Jas. 1:13-15

4. Is God responsible for natural evils as a judgment upon

moral evil?

| Gen. 3:16-19 | Is. 45:7-9 | Rom. 8:20 |

5. Summarize this section answering the question, Is God the author of evil?

D. What God has done about evil

1. Why has God allowed such evils as war, illness, pollution and violence?

Num. 14:27-33	Ps. 107:17	Lam. 1:5
Deut. 7:1-4	Is. 24:5-6	Neh. 9:26-27
(cf. Gen. 15:16)	Jer. 4:18-19	Acts 5:1-11
Deut. 8:19-20	Jer. 13:22	1 Cor. 11:29-30

2. In what way has God shown his concern for suffering man?

Is. 63:9	Lk. 24:46	Heb. 9:26
Hos. 3:1	Heb. 2:10, 14-18	Heb. 13:12
Mt. 10:29-31		

3. Explain man's responsibility and God's responsibility for the injustice of Christ's death at Calvary and the marvelous provision of the cross for salvation.

Acts 4:23-28

4. What does God call upon believers in Christ to do for the cause of righteousness in a fallen world?

Phil. 1:29	Heb. 11:26	1 Pet. 3:14
2 Thess. 1:5	Heb. 11:36-38	1 Pet. 4:16
2 Tim. 2:9	1 Pet. 2:19, 21	

5. How does God overrule suffering and evil for beneficial purposes? What good comes from evil in these verses?

Gen. 50:20	Jn. 9:1-3	Rom. 5:3-4
Job 1:8-12, 20-21	Jn. 11:5-6, 11, 15	Phil. 1:12
Job 2:3-6	Jn. 11:38-45	1 Cor. 9:25-27
Ps. 119:67, 71	Jn. 15:2	2 Cor. 12:8-10
Mt. 8:23-27	Acts 8:1-4	Phil. 3:10

6. Summarize this section by answering these questions: Is all suffering a judgment upon specific sins? What other reasons are there for suffering?

E. What God will do about evil

1. Will evil endlessly continue to disrupt good?

| Rom. 8:18-25 | Rev. 11:15-18 | Rev. 20:1-3, 7-15 |
| 2 Pet. 3:7-12 | Rev. 19:1-2, 11-21 | Rev. 21:8 |

2. In the face of multiplying evils, on what basis can we expect the triumph of righteousness?

2 Pet. 2:1-10   2 Pet. 3:2, 7-13

3. What will the ultimate state of unqualified goodness be like?

2 Pet. 3:13   Rev. 21:1-7   Rev. 21:22—22:15

4. How will the evils experienced in one's entire life on earth compare with the good awaiting God's people in eternity?

Is. 54:8   Rom. 8:18   2 Cor. 4:8-18
Mt. 5:12

5. Summarize this section (as well as Section D) by answering the question, Why doesn't God do something about the tragic evils in the world?

IV. Conclusion

Formulate an answer to the question "Why is there so much suffering in the world?" Is God both good and all-powerful? Show why you reject other explanations and accept the stance you are adopting.[10]

V. Relevance

A. If God were to deal decisively with all the sin of men today, would you yourself be ready for this?

B. While there is much that we do not know about any particular tragedy, Albertus Pieters has said, "The little that we do know is more valid for our interpretation of the world than the much we do not know." Apply what you have learned to a concrete situation: How would you talk with the parents of an infant who is permanently crippled at birth? Or what could you say to parents whose child had died in a hospital nursery because he was fed a formula into which salt was mistakenly mixed instead of sugar?

Notes

[1] Edward John Carnell, "Evil: Why?" *Eternity,* December 1960, p. 23.

[2] Ninian Smart, "Indian Philosophy," *Encyclopedia of Philosophy,* ed. Paul Edwards (New York: The Macmillan Company and the Free Press, 1967), IV, p. 159.

[3] Mary Baker Eddy, *Science and Health with Key to the Scriptures* (Boston: First Church of Christ, Scientist, 1932), pp. 472-73.

[4] Ninian Smart, "Zoroastrianism," *Encyclopedia of Philosophy,* ed. Paul Edwards (New York: The Macmillan Company and the Free Press, 1967), VIII, p. 382.

[5] John Stuart Mill, *Essays on Ethics, Religion and Society,* Vol. X of *Collected Works of John Stuart Mill* (Canada: University of Toronto Press, 1969), p. 455.

[6] T. L. Osborn, *Divine Healing* (Tulsa: Evangelist T. L. Osborn, 1949), I, pp. 1-78.

[7] John Hick, "Evil, The Problem of," *Encyclopedia of Philosophy,* ed. Paul Edwards (New York: The Macmillan Company and the Free Press, 1967), III, pp. 138-39; and John Hick, *Evil and the God of Love* (London: Collins, 1968), especially pp. 207-400.

[8] C. S. Lewis, *The Problem of Pain* (New York: The Macmillan Company, 1948), pp. 1-145; William Fitch, *God and Evil* (Grand Rapids: Wm. B. Eerdmans, 1967), pp. 1-183; Gordon R. Lewis, "Suffering," "Temptation," *Zondervan Pictorial Bible Encyclopedia,* ed. Merrill Tenney (Grand Rapids: Zondervan, forthcoming); Hugh Silvester, *Arguing with God* (Downers Grove, Ill.: InterVarsity Press, 1971), pp. 1-128.

[9] For a helpful interpretation of the biblical materials on the origin of sin see Francis A. Schaeffer, *Genesis in Space and Time* (Downers Grove, Ill.: InterVarsity Press, 1972), pp. 1-101.

[10] It would be instructive to compare your conclusion here with that in *Decide for Yourself,* study 8.

What's the purpose of miracles?

4

"Are miracles possible?"

"Is anything inexplicable a miracle?"

"Are there occult miracles?"

"Can the living communicate with the spirits of the dead?"

"Do the stars influence our lives?"

"Can we really predict anything about the future?"

"Was Christ's resurrection just a freakish event in a wide-open universe in which anything can happen?"

"What about charismatic gifts of the Holy Spirit—speaking in tongues and divine healing?"

"How does one account for healings in a non-Christian context?"

"What is the place of miracles in Christian experience today?"

I. The Problem

Experiencing "future shock" because of many novel and unexpected developments, people are now asking serious questions about matters they previously dismissed lightly. Many people are no longer troubled by whether miracles are possible; rather, they are asking what their significance is. Few recent writers imagine that they live in a neat, completely predictable, surprise-free world. At any time a person may come face to face with the unexpected. With Peter Berger, the sociologist-theologian, many think that "human life gains the greatest part of its richness from . . . any experience of stepping outside the take-for-granted reality of everyday life, any openness to the mystery that surrounds us on all sides."[1]

This study assumes enough openness on the part of the reader to consider a world-view which accounts for both the uniformities and novelties of human experience—the uniformities caused by the usual acts of divine providence and the genuine novelties caused by the extraordinary acts of beings superior to man.

To believe in God is to believe in the possibility of miracles. C. S. Lewis wrote, "But if we admit God, must we admit miracles? Indeed, indeed, you have no security against it. That is the bargain. Theology says to you in effect, 'Admit God and with Him the risk of a few miracles, and I in turn will ratify your faith in the uniformity as regards the overwhelming majority of events.' The philosophy which forbids you to make uniformity absolute is also the philosophy which offers you solid ground for believing it to be general, to be *almost* absolute."[2]

A part of the problem of this study is to derive a definition of *miracle* from the study of evidence. At this point, however, a working definition may be of value. A miracle may be defined as an observable phenomenon, inexplicable in terms of natural forces or sequences of events (a "mighty act"), so extraordinary as to elicit awe (a "wonder") and indicative of a power acting upon nature for good or evil purposes (a "sign"). The reader may want to revise this definition in his conclusion. When *miracle* is used only of divine acts, the purposes can be made more explicit.

Another problem is to achieve some objectivity in surveying claims for the miraculous and some discernment in evaluating them by a personal study of relevant biblical teaching.

II. Live Options

A. Mysterious influences from the arrangement of the planets and stars at the time of an individual's birth decisively affect his character and enable him to predict the otherwise unknown future. Because reality is orderly, changes in the stars effect changes in the destiny of individuals and societies on earth.[3] (Astrology)

B. Communication with the spirits of the dead brings comfort to the sorrowing and hidden knowledge about the future. The existence of evil spirits is acknowledged, but the emphasis falls on contact with good spirits and obedience to the golden rule in order to achieve harmony with the universe.[4] (Spiritualism)

C. Traditionally, extraordinary tragedies indicate the importance of the most powerful source of evil—Satan. He can do great harm to those who refuse to worship him. For some recent movements, Satan is not an external object of worship but merely a symbol for the material world and sensual pleasure.[5] (Satanism)

D. Through magic a sorcerer, a medicine man or an image of one's enemy can bring harm to an adversary. The worship of spirits protects the faithful from the curse charms of magicians.[6] (Voodooism)

E. Since the fall of angels and men, the battle has raged between good and evil not only on earth, but also in spiritual realms. God's temporal purposes for the world may be achieved through the ordinary activities of men and the functions of nature. But the opposition to God's moral and spiritual purposes is so persistent from Satanic influences and fallen human nature that no merely natural development can restore fallen creatures to the fellowship and service of God. "Signs," "wonders" and "mighty acts" occur not to satisfy curiosity about one's future, but to rescue fallen man from evil by "direct corrective acts."[7] Hence the majority of biblical miracles occur during times of crisis in the battle with evil. Clusters of miracles happened as Moses led God's people out of Egyptian slavery, Elijah and Elisha defeated the prophets of Baal, Christ provided atonement for the sin of the world and the apostles planted the church. Some miracles occurred at other times as well. (Generally all of these are to be distinguished from the divine regeneration of the human heart and answers to prayer which do not constitute visible evidence in nature.)

Among those who agree on this view differences emerge on the purpose and role of publicly observable miracles in the Christian life today.

1. Some expect no miracles in the world today. Such "signs" were for the single purpose of validating an agent of revelation (a prophet, Jesus Christ or an apostle). With the completion of the New Testament revelation, the need for further display of miraculous works ceased. No more men can meet the qualifications of an apostle (to have been with Christ throughout his ministry and to have witnessed his post-resurrection appearances). So at the end of the first century no more sign-gifts were given. The "temporary" gifts of apostleship, prophecy, miracles, healing, speaking in tongues, interpretation of tongues and the discerning of spirits have no place in the Christian life today.[8]

2. Others expect all these gifts to be as prominent today as

in New Testament times, or even more prominent. On this view, sign-gifts serve not only to accredit revelational agents but also to build up the church, the body of Christ. Emphasis usually falls on speaking in tongues to confirm the baptism of the Holy Spirit and upon healing to provide the physical wholeness Christ provided. Whatever may be the place of the other sign-gifts, tongues and healing are given a prominent role in every Christian's life today.[9]

3. A third group neither gives prominence to the sign-gifts nor forbids them, but allows for their bestowal and use in a manner, and for purposes, consistent with God's integrated program of revelation and redemption. Because of indications of direct demonic influence in human life today, this group does not think it strange for God to act in direct ways to liberate people from these evil powers. Because the Holy Spirit gives gifts to believers as he wills, Christians are not to seek the sign-gifts nor to make any of them mandatory for all. Tongues is not a normal sign of the Spirit's baptism to be experienced by all believers. Though in the resurrected state believers will have perfect health, no promise of Scripture holds out complete freedom from illness in the present life. Claims to possess gifts like healing or tongues cannot be accepted uncritically. These phenomena are found in religions and cults which contradict the central message of the Scripture. They have been misused in Christian churches which preach the gospel. Spirit-given and Spirit-exercised gifts are consistent with the teaching of Scripture and the edification of the church; they do not divide the church but build it up in love. A scale of values is crucial: Christians are not to be preoccupied with gifts and miracles. Kurt Koch said, "In the New Testament healing and forgiveness are bound together, and it is forgiveness that takes pride of place."[10]

III. Debated Issues and Biblical Data
A. The warfare of Satan against God

1. What are the purposes of the Satanic kingdom which opposes Christ?

Mt. 13:19, 38-39	2 Cor. 4:3-4	1 Pet. 5:8
Jn. 8:44	2 Cor. 11:13-15	1 Jn. 3:8
Acts 10:38	Eph. 2:2	Rev. 12:9, 17
Acts 13:10	Eph. 6:12	

2. Has Satan the power to enable his followers to perform great signs and wonders among men?

Mt. 12:22-29	2 Thess. 2:9-12	Rev. 13:1-4, 11-15
Mt. 24:24		

3. What are the sources of unusual spiritistic phenomena?

Acts 16:16-18	Gal. 5:19-20	1 Tim. 4:1-3

4. What did Saul's attempt to contact the spirit of Samuel through the witch of Endor show about God's view of spiritualism?

1 Sam. 28:3-25	1 Chron. 10:13-14

5. How serious was it in Bible times to consult the spirits for guidance?

Lev. 19:31	Lev. 20:27	1 Cor. 10:14-22
Lev. 20:6	Deut. 18:9-14	

6. How reliable is guidance from astrology?

Is. 47:13-15	Dan. 2:27-28	Dan. 5:7-15
Jer. 10:1-3	Dan. 4:7	

7. Where can people find reliable guidance concerning the future?

Deut. 29:29	2 Tim. 3:15-17	2 Pet. 1:19-21
Is. 8:19-22	Jas. 1:5-8	

8. Summarize this section by evaluating the success with which astrology, spiritualism and Satanism can achieve their intended functions over long periods of time.

B. Extraordinary acts of God to redeem men from evil

1. Although God works providentially in everything that comes to pass,[11] what were God's purposes in his unusual working with Israel under Moses and Joshua?

Ex. 3:19-20	Ex. 9:14-16, 29	Josh. 4:23-24
Ex. 4:1-9	Ex. 14:31	Josh. 5:1

Ex. 7:1-5, 17   Josh. 3:10-11   Ps. 106:9-12

2. Why did God perform mighty acts in the time of Elijah and Elisha?

1 Kings 17:17-24   1 Kings 18:17-40   2 Kings 5:14-15

3. Why did Jesus Christ perform miracles?

Mk. 2:9-12	Jn. 2:11	Jn. 11:4, 40-42
Lk. 4:17-21	Jn. 5:36	Jn. 20:30-31
Lk. 18:42-43	Jn. 10:37-38	

4. For what reasons was Jesus Christ raised from the dead?

Mt. 28:9, 16-20	Acts 10:36-43	1 Cor. 15:20-28
Lk. 24:6-7, 25-27	Acts 13:26-39	1 Cor. 15:56-58
Lk. 24:45-47	Acts 17:30-31	Eph. 1:20-23
Jn. 20:19-31	Acts 26:23	Eph. 4:7-16
Acts 2:22-36	Rom. 1:4	Col. 1:18-20
Acts 3:15, 17-26		

5. What purposes were evident in the miracles of the apostles?

Acts 2:11, 37-47	Acts 8:14-17	1 Cor. 12:7
Acts 3:1-16	Acts 10:44-48	1 Cor. 14:12
Acts 4:8-12, 29-33	Acts 14:3	Heb. 2:1-4
Acts 5:12-16	Rom. 15:14-19	

(In the Acts 8 and 10 accounts, it is helpful to understand that the Jews had long been at odds with both Samaritans and Gentiles.)

6. Summarize this section by indicating the essential purposes of biblical miracles in the great periods of their manifestation.

C. The role of miracles today

1. Evaluate the strength of the case that miracles ceased with the last of the first-century apostles. (Live option E1)

Acts 1:21-22   1 Cor. 13:8

The immediate end for which they [miracles] were given is not left doubtful, and that proves to be not directly the extension of the church, but the authentication of the Apostles as messengers from God. . . .

The charismata belonged, in a true sense, to the Apostles, and constituted one of the signs of an Apostle. Only in the two great initial instances of the descent of the Spirit at Pentecost and the reception of Cornelius are charismata recorded as conferred without the laying on of the hands of Apostles. There is no instance on record of their conference by the laying on of the hands of any one else than an Apostle. . . . It could not be more emphatically stated that the Holy Spirit was conferred by the laying on of the hands, specifically of the Apostles, and of the Apostles alone (Acts 8:14-17). . . . Hermann Cremer is quite right when he says that "the Apostolic charismata bear the same relation to those of the ministry that the Apostolic office does to the pastoral office"; the extraordinary gifts belonged to the extraordinary office and showed themselves only in connection with its activities.

. . . It [this view] explains the unobserved dying out of these gifts. It even explains—what might at first sight seem inconsistent with it—the failure of allusion to them in the first half of the second century. The great missionary Apostles, Paul and Peter, had passed away by A.D. 68, and apparently only John was left in extreme old age until the last decade of the first century. The number of those upon whom the hands of Apostles had been laid, living still in the second century, cannot have been very large. . . . Miracles do not appear on the page of Scripture vagrantly, here and there, and elsewhere indifferently, without assignable reason. They belong to revelation periods, and appear only when God is speaking to His people through accredited messengers, declaring His gracious purposes. . . .

And when this historic process of organic revelation had reached its completeness, and when the whole knowledge of God designed for the saving health of the world had been incorporated into the living body of the world's thought—there remained, of course, no further revelation to be made, and there has been accordingly no further revelation made. God the Holy Spirit has made it his subsequent work, not to introduce new and unneeded revelations into the world, but to diffuse this one complete revelation through the world, and to bring mankind into the saving knowledge of it. [Subsequently, alleged miracles and speaking in tongues are attributed to hysteria and faith-healings to natural mind-cures or other natural causes.][12]

2. Evaluate the arguments used to justify a present expectation of as many, or more, miracles as in the time of the apostles. (Live option E2)

| Mt. 8:17 | Jn. 14:12 | Jas. 5:14-15 |
| Mk. 16:17-18[13] | Acts 6:5, 8[14] | Heb. 13:8 |

[Admittedly,] raising the dead is no where promised as a privilege or possibility for the believers of to-day. There is, indeed, in one instance, Matt. x:8, a command to raise the dead; but this was given specifically *to the twelve* and in a temporary commission. It therefore differs very materially from the promise in Mark xvi, which was to *all believers*, and is contained in a commission which was for the entire dispensation of the Spirit. That the Lord did this miracle, and that his apostles did it, in one or two instances is not enough. Unless we can show some specific promise given to the church as a whole we are bound to concede that such works are not for us or for our age. Healing the sick, on the contrary, rests on a distinct and specific promise to believers.

[Healings are attested throughout the history of the church, in the works of theologians, in the ministries of missionaries and in the experience of a number of the author's (A. J. Gordon's) contemporaries.]

Is it right for us to pray to God to perform a miracle of healing in our behalf? "The truth is," answers one eminent writer, "that to ask God to act at all, and to ask him to perform a miracle are one and the same thing." That is to say, a miracle is the immediate action of God, as distinguished from his mediate action, through natural laws. We see no reason, therefore, why we should hesitate to pray for the healing of our bodies any more than for the renewal of our souls. Both are miracles; but both are covered and provided for by the same clear word of promise.[15]

3. Evaluate the support for the view that miracles did not cease with the apostles, are not to be expected routinely in the Christian life, but may occur on occasions of special need for deliverance from demonic influence in connection with confession of sin and faith in Christ. The charismatic gifts and power for their use are given sovereignly by the Holy Spirit as he wills. In any case, they must be exercised in love for the building up of the church. (Live option E3)

1 Cor. 12:4-11, 27-31   Eph. 4:7-13   1 Pet. 4:10-11
1 Cor. 14:39

[Since evidence shows that some miracles occurred in Bible history apart from the clusters at the time of the Exodus, Elijah-Elisha and the New Testament (for example, Gen. 6; Gen. 19:24-26; Judg. 6:27-40; 1 Sam. 5:1-12; 2 Sam. 6:6-7; 2 Kings 19:35; 2 Chron. 26:16-21; Dan. 3:19-27; Dan. 6:16-23; Jn. 2:1-10), so some miracles may occur in this age apart from the purpose of authenticating apostles at the founding of the church.]

We must remember then, that the most important problem facing us is not the health of our bodies but rather the forgiveness of our sins. We find the same emphasis in James 5:14-19 where confession of sin is recommended whenever healing of the body is sought. . . .

In the Scriptures the order is always: the soul's welfare, then that of the body. . . . So then, forgiveness is essential, healing a possibility.

Events of this nature [the healing of a Biafran man whose lungs were full of blood, by a prayer for deliverance from the powers of darkness] are nothing we can copy. God cannot be forced to do the same for all who are suffering in this way. He alone is sovereign. It is he, and not us, who decides who is to be healed and who is not. And above all we must never fall into the trap of believing that just because God has acted in this way once, we can now start commanding the powers of darkness at the bedside of every sick person, as is frequently the habit of members of certain extreme sects.

In the majority of cases confession and forgiveness are the basic conditions determining whether God will act in any further way on behalf of a person who is physically or mentally ill.[16]

4. Summarize this section by drawing your conclusion about the role of the miraculous in Christian experience today. Indicate your reasons for it.

D. Criteria by which to test claims for the miraculous

1. What criteria did God give to Israel through Moses for distinguishing a true prophet from a false one?

Deut. 13:1-5   Deut. 18:15-22

2. What were the tests of authentic apostles?

Acts 1:21-22   2 Cor. 12:12   1 Jn. 4:1-3
Gal. 1:8-9

3. What regulations were necessarily met if speaking in tongues in public was of the Holy Spirit?[17]

1 Cor. 12:3, 7   1 Cor. 14:26-28   1 Cor. 14:33-34, 40
1 Cor. 12:31—13:2

4. Some writers have pointed out that claims for a miraculous healing cannot be established as true unless it can be shown that the healing did not occur for one of the following reasons: (a) The disease or sickness had run its course; (b) God's blessing was on medical skill, surgical skill or other means; (c) the power of the mind was exerted over the body, that is, the cure was psychosomatic; (d) the healer influenced the sufferer through hypnotism, mesmerism or strong willpower; (e) Satanic or demonic force was responsible.[18]

5. Summarize this section by indicating how you would apply the biblical tests to alleged miracle workers today.

E. Resources and responsibilities

1. What resources are available and what responsibilities

must be acknowledged as Christians face the forces of evil today?

Mt. 17:14-21	Eph. 6:10-18	1 Pet. 5:8-9
Acts 16:18	2 Tim. 2:23-26	1 Jn. 4:4; 5:5
Eph. 4:27	Jas. 4:7	

2. Summarize this section by showing the essential aspects of spiritual fortification against influences from the demonic realm.

IV. Conclusion

Formulate an answer to the question "What's the purpose of miracles?" by pulling together your summaries of the previous sections, evaluating the live options (II) with which you differ and interacting with any reading you have done in the sources listed in the notes below.

V. Relevance

A. In the *Screwtape Letters*, C. S. Lewis said, "There are two equal and opposite errors into which our race can fall about the devils. One is to disbelieve in their existence. The other is to believe, and to feel an excessive and unhealthy interest in them. They themselves are equally pleased by both errors and hail a materialist or a magician with the same delight."[19] Into which of these errors are you most naturally inclined to fall? What have you gained from this study to help counteract this?

B. Suggest some reasons why God does not grant miracle-working power to all who desire it. (For example, what appeal do you think it would have for those who refuse to accept personal responsibility for their lives?)

C. Evaluate the following statement from the standpoint of your own attitudes as a result of your study:

A healthy mind, full of faith in God's power and in God's wisdom, without denying that "sign" miracles may occur when God so chooses, expects to learn foreign languages by regular processes of study and hard work. A healthy

Christian mind expects to observe the ordinary principles of bodily health and sanitation, using such physical provisions of food, shelter, and medicine as divine providence may make available. In spreading the Gospel one does expect the convicting ministry of the Spirit and the evidence of transformed lives, but one does not expect, unless God should so choose, that the sudden healing of a man born with twisted feet and ankle bones, will gather a crowd to hear us preach the Word. He is prepared to serve the Lord, to experience wonderful answers to prayer, and to find that the Word does not return void, regardless of "signs and wonders."[20]

Notes

[1] Peter Berger, *A Rumor of Angels* (Garden City, N. Y.: Doubleday, 1969), p. 94.

[2] C. S. Lewis, *Miracles* (New York: The Macmillan Company, 1948), p. 128. This book's entire discussion of the possibility of miracles is recommended.

[3] Joseph Bayly, *What About Horoscopes?* (Elgin, Ill.: David C. Cook, 1970), pp. 1-95; E. W. Maunder, "Astrology," *International Standard Bible Encyclopedia,* ed. James Orr (Grand Rapids: Wm. B. Eerdmans, 1949), I, pp. 295-300.

[4] James Bjornstad, *Twentieth Century Prophecy: Jeane Dixon, Edgar Cayce* (Minneapolis: Bethany Fellowship, 1969), pp. 1-155; Victor H. Ernest, *I Talked with Spirits* (Wheaton, Ill.: Tyndale House, 1970), pp. 1-89; Gordon R. Lewis, *Confronting the Cults* (Philadelphia: Presbyterian and Reformed, 1966), pp. 163-98.

[5] Arthur Lyons, *The Second Coming: Satanism in America* (New York: Dodd, Mead & Co., 1970), pp. 1-211.

[6] Harmon Hartzell Bro, "Voodoo," *Encyclopedia Britannica,* Vol. 23 (Chicago: William Benton, 1968), p. 122.

[7] Benjamin B. Warfield, "Christian Supernaturalism," in *Biblical and Theological Studies,* ed. Samuel G. Craig (Philadelphia: Presbyterian and Reformed, 1952), pp. 1-21; Richard C. Trench, *Notes on the Miracles of Our Lord* (New York: D. Appleton and Co., 1873), pp. 1-103.

[8] Benjamin B. Warfield, *Miracles: Yesterday and Today* (Grand Rapids: Wm. B. Eerdmans, 1965), pp. 1-327; John F. Walvoord, *The Holy Spirit* (Findlay, Ohio: Dunham, 1954), pp. 163-88.

[9] A. J. Gordon, *The Ministry of Healing* (Boston: Howard Gannett, 1883), pp. 1-249; Kathryn Kuhlman, *I Believe in Miracles* (New York: Pyramid Books, 1969), pp. 1-223; Nils Block-Hoell, *The Pentecostal Movement: Its Origin, Development, and Distinctive Character* (New York: Humanities Press, 1964), pp. 141-51.

[10] Kurt Koch, *Occult Bondage and Deliverance: Advice for Counselling the Sick, the Troubled and the Occultly Oppressed* (Grand Rapids: Kregel, 1970), pp. 1-198; Kurt Koch, *Between Christ and Satan* (Grand Rapids: Kregel, 1970), pp. 1-191; J. O. Buswell, Jr., *A Systematic Theology of the Christian Religion* (Grand Rapids: Zondervan, 1962), I, pp. 176-82.

[11] S. I. McMillen, *None of These Diseases* (Old Tappan, N. J.: Fleming H. Revell, 1963), pp. 1-158; Gordon R. Lewis, *Decide for Yourself: A Theological Workbook* (Downers Grove, Ill.: InterVarsity Press, 1970), pp. 63-67.

[12] Warfield, *Miracles, pp. 21-26.*

[13] A problem exists here. Many scholars do not believe the verses identified as Mark 16:9-20 actually belong to the Gospel of Mark. The RSV, for instance, prints these verses in italics apart from the main body of the text, prefacing them with the comment, "Other texts and versions add as Mark 16:9-20 the following passage."

[14] Stephen was not an apostle.

[15] Gordon, pp. 53, 193.

[16] Koch, *Occult Bondage and Deliverance,* pp. 76-81.

[17] See John R. W. Stott, *The Baptism and Fullness of the Holy Spirit* (Downers Grove, Ill.: InterVarsity Press, 1964), pp. 1-60; Anthony A. Hoekema, *What About Tongue-Speaking?* (Grand Rapids: Wm. B. Eerdmans, 1966), pp. 1-161.

[18] Ada R. Habershon, *The Study of Miracles* (Grand Rapids: Kregel, 1957), p. 243;

Vincent Edmunds and C. Gordon Scorer, *Some Thoughts on Faith Healing* (London: The Tyndale Press, 1956), pp. 1-72.

[19] C. S. Lewis, *The Screwtape Letters* (New York: The Macmillan Company, 1943), p. 9.

[20] J. Oliver Buswell, Jr., "Miracles," in *Zondervan Pictorial Bible Dictionary* (Grand Rapids: Zondervan, 1963), p. 546.

Why are there so many hypocrites in the Christian church?

5

"Why are so many church members phonies?"

"If Christianity is so great, why do some Christians live decidedly non-Christian lives?"

"Why should I consider Christ when the church is full of hypocrites?"

"Why are there so many divisions among Christians?"

"Is the institutional church really Christian?"

"Why don't more so-called Christian churches get involved in meeting the social needs of their communities—ecology, race, ghettoes, the starving?"

"Isn't Christianity a white man's religion?"

"Why does the so-called Christian community turn its back on long hairs and try to make them conform rather than accepting them and loving them?"

I. The Problem

Tired of superficial, materialistic institutions, people properly turn to religion for reality. All too often, however, they are disillusioned with what they see in the lives of Christians and in the church. From the ruins of shattered ideals, a chorus of outcries is heard. Most of us cannot help but identify with at least some of these feelings as a result of unfortunate experiences of our own. If our indignation is not aroused by pious pretense in the name of Christ, we may be hopelessly cynical. At the same time, we must be aware of the gravity of judging another to be hypocritical.

Part of the problem of this entire study is to determine the meaning of hypocrisy. For our present purposes, we will work with this definition: "Hypocrisy is incompatibility between what one is and what one pretends or believes himself to be. . . . Hypocrisy is the normal outcome of sin by which man believes in that which is not and believes himself to be what he is not."[1] Hypocrisy is a conflict involving at least two of these three: (1) being a Christian, (2) saying one is a Christian and (3) living as a Christian. The discrepancy between character, word and action may be conscious or unconscious.[2] Sincerity may or may not be present.

The assumption of this study is that those who raise serious questions, such as those listed on page 62, are not merely registering a complaint, but are determined enough to search for some contributing factors. The primary source of information on authentic and inauthentic religion is the Bible. The student is asked to examine for himself some of its key passages on hypocrisy and draw his own conclusions about the immediate reasons and the root cause of so much religious duplicity.

Before examining the Scriptures, the reader is asked to survey the extensive thought given to the subject of hypocrisy by a number of influential writers. These possible explanations are then to be tested by the biblical evidence and his own experience.

II. Live Options

A. Bertrand Russell, the English philosopher, attributed hypocrisy to an unrealistic desire to be "nice." In a satirical essay he says "Nice People" are protected from crude contact with reality; dishonestly seek to improve upon reality; are shocked by the naked truth; preserve illusions of grandeur for politicians, educators and religious leaders; defend Victorian standards in education; suspect pleasure wherever they see it; and hate life as manifested in tendencies of cooperation, the boisterousness of children, and expressions of sex, with which their imaginations are obsessed. "In a word, nice people are those who have nasty minds."[3]

B. In the assessment of Keith Miller, a primary reason for hypocrisy is a craving for acceptance to the point of dishonesty. It is not so much that people lie, but they do not press the truth when it might hurt church leaders or someone else's feelings. Being honest seems cruel or tactless. The drive for social acceptance and conformity leads to a subtle duplicity. Because Christians fear rejection, they may become dishonest with themselves (pretending to be unselfish). They are afraid that if people find out what they are really like they will not be accepted. Yet everyone knows that Christians also are subject to the weaknesses that are universal. The church is not a fellowship of former sinners, but a community of forgiveness.[4]

C. Francis Schaeffer thinks that hypocrisy in Christians may be traced to a lack of internal compassion and visible love for those they purport to love. Both liberal and conservative churches seem to be merely mouthing words about love. There is no use saying you have community if it does not get down to the "tough stuff" of life. The world will not listen if we have right doctrine and right polity but are not exhibiting community: "The observable and practical love of our days certainly should without reservation cut across all such lines as language, nationalities, national frontiers, younger or older, colors of skin, education and economic levels, accent, line of birth, the class system of our particular locality, dress, short and long hair among whites and African and non-African hairdos among blacks, the wearing of shoes and non-wearing of shoes, cultural differentiations, and the more traditional and less traditional forms of worship."[5]

D. Schaeffer also finds hypocrisy when the actual beliefs of a person or institution are incompatible with its advertized beliefs. Many so-called Christian churches fail to practice an orthodoxy of community in the visible church. Leaders and members of many churches deny the basic Christian realities: a personal God who is there, the historic Christ, the Bible as the verbalized Word of God and the way of salvation by grace through faith. Whether in the name of liberalism, progressivism or humanism, taking the name of the Christian God and denying him in practice is as heinous as marital infidelity. The biblical prophets called it spiritual adultery.[6]

E. According to John A. Mackay, hypocrisy may occur because people yield to the temptation to transform orthodox concepts into the realities themselves. Loyalty to ideas about the Bible, about God, about Jesus Christ and about other Christian realities becomes a substitute for loyalty to God, the Bible and Jesus Christ—and also for authentic Christian behavior. Theological concepts are important and necessary to depict reality and to clarify its nature, but they do not constitute the reality itself. A man can say, "I believe the Bible from cover to cover" without taking seriously what the Bible says. Whenever ideas, of whatever kind, are given the status of being the ultimate object of Christian devotion, they become idols and their affirmation is an act of hypocrisy.[7]

F. Arnold Praeter says phoniness occurs because people feel they should call Jesus Christ their Lord but insist on running their own lives. Pride has replaced humility, and people are no longer driven to grace to be made whole. They no longer see themselves as objects of mercy, grace and love. They worship themselves. Having fallen into the trap of self-justification, they merely seek self-improvement, not a self made new.[8] Loyalty to a person, an organization or a social and political order, John Mackay explains, may take precedence over loyalty to Christ and his kingdom.[9]

G. Mackay also points out that some may be tempted to claim an experience with God that they have not in fact had. So they may identify vital experience of God with attendance at a church service. They attend not as true worshippers but to get a thrill or to maintain an image for personal or public reasons. They are Christians in appearance but not in reality. Membership in an institutional church becomes a substitute for a personal relationship to God and for effective membership in the family of God.[10]

H. Christians may champion ecclesiastical interests, Dietrich Bonhoeffer observed, but be unwilling to take any risks in the service of humanity. What do Christians believe in such a way as to stake their whole lives upon it? It is not enough to speak of the church's faith; Christians need their own vital faith. A strong line must be taken against pride, power-worship, envy and humbug.[11] The affectation of Christianity may be the result of preaching cheap grace. Cheap grace is the preaching of forgiveness without requiring repentance, baptism without church discipline, communion without confession, absolution without contrition. Cheap grace is grace without discipleship, grace without the cross, grace without Jesus Christ, living and incarnate.[12]

Innumerable times a whole Christian community has broken down because it has sprung from a wish-dream. The serious Christian set down for the first time in a Christian community is likely to bring with him a very definite idea of what Christian life together should be and try to realize it. But God's grace speedily shatters such dreams. He who loves his dream of community more than the Christian community itself becomes a destroyer of the latter, even though his personal intentions may be ever so honest and earnest and sacrificial. God hates visionary dreaming; it makes the dreamer proud and pretentious. The man who fashions a visionary community demands that it be realized by God, by others and by himself. He enters the community of Christians with his demands, sets up his own law and judges both his brethren and God himself accordingly. He stands adamant, a living reproach to all others in the circle of brethren. He acts as if he is the creator of Christian community, as if his dream binds men together. When things do not go his way, he calls the effort a failure. When his ideal picture is destroyed, he sees the community going to ruin. So he becomes first an accuser of the brethren, then an accuser of God and finally the despairing accuser of himself.[13]

I. The institutional church gives false profession, said Reinhold Niebuhr, when it ceases to be the servant of Christ and makes Christ the servant of the church.[14] Then a universal self-deception occurs consciously or unconsciously—the identification of the institution's special interests with general interests and universal values.[15] This happens in social and political realms, as well as the sphere of the church. Egoism, the predominant inclination of human nature, combines with greed and the will to power to lift one's own interests all out of proportion to their importance.[16]

James Kavanaugh, as a priest, sought for years to defend what seemed to him such a system. He said, "Daily my anguish grew as I recognized the unholy limits that arrogant and unfounded laws had put on God." So Kavanaugh left his church, which in place of love, he thought, offered needy people a legalism grown arrogant and inhumane.[17] Some Protestants have observed a similar tendency. Edward John Carnell wrote: "While we must be solicitous about doctrine,

Scripture says that our primary business is love. But the fundamentalist finds the first task much more inviting than the second. Despite the severest apostolic warnings, schism in the church is often interpreted as a sign of Christian virtue. Separation promotes status in the cult; unity through love does not."[18] Again, "While the world is offended by the physical divisions in the church, the *real* offense is the manner in which these divisions are used as vehicles of pride and pretense. . . . It is a compromise, made far too lightly, between Christianity and the world. . . . It represents the accommodation of Christianity to the caste system of human society. It carries over into the organization of the Christian principle of brotherhood the prides and prejudices, the privileges and prestige, as well as the humiliations and abasements, the injustices and inequalities of that specious order of high and low wherein men find the satisfaction of their craving for vainglory."[19]

J. Misrepresenting the nature of genuine Christianity, some church leaders avoid the suffering required by opposition to the world and simply play church, in the judgment of Soren Kierkegaard. There is no more danger in their role in Christendom than in the imaginary war in which a child plays soldier.[20] Under the guise of perfecting Christianity, they make it its opposite. They designate as the Christianity of the New Testament that which is not the Christianity of the New Testament.[21] Instead of obedience to God's will, they do their own will in the name of God. Weddings, baptisms and "worship" services are filled with ludicrous twaddle.[22] They make much ado about being like Christ was centuries ago, but have no contemporaneous willingness to suffer any inconvenience to serve others.[23] Their primary concern is not God but the public. They apply Christianity tranquilizingly to be completely like the millions.[24] People in Christendom are like the heir of a fortune which has a requirement he does not like. He takes the fortune and says good day to the obligation. People like to take the gift of

Christianity and say good day to the obligation.[25]

K. According to Blaise Pascal, all forms of hypocrisy may be traced ultimately to the corruption of human nature since the Fall. "There are different degrees of aversion to truth; but all may perhaps be said to have it in some degree, because it is inseparable from self-love. . . . Hence it happens that if any have some interest in being loved by us, they are averse to render us a service which they know to be disagreeable. They treat us as we wish to be treated. We hate the truth, and they hide it from us. We desire flattery, and they flatter us. We like to be deceived, and they deceive us. . . . Human life is thus only a perpetual illusion; men deceive and flatter each other. No one speaks of us in our presence as he does of us in our absence. . . . Man is then only disguise, falsehood, and hypocrisy, both in himself and in regard to others. He does not wish anyone to tell him the truth; he avoids telling it to others, and *all these dispositions, so removed from justice and reason, have a natural root in his heart.*"[26]

An internal war in man between reason and the passions leaves man in constant strife. He is always divided against and opposed to himself.[27] It is vain to seek the remedy within man himself. "Your chief maladies are pride, which takes you away from God, and lust, which binds you to the earth; and they [the philosophers] have done nothing else but cherish one or the other of these diseases. If they gave you God as an end, it was only to administer to your pride; they made you think that you are by nature like Him, and conformed to Him. And those who saw the absurdity of this claim put you on another precipice, by making you understand that your nature was like that of the brutes, and led you to seek your good in the lusts which are shared by animals. This is not the way to cure you of your unrighteousness, which these wise men knew."[28] Again, "From lust men have found and extracted excellent rules of policy, morality and justice; but in reality this vile root of man, this *figmentum malum*, is only covered, it is not taken away."[29] "Men never do evil so completely and cheerfully as when they do it from religious conviction."[30] So "the Christian religion teaches men these two truths; that there is a God whom men can know, and that there is a corruption in their nature which renders them unworthy of Him."[31]

III. Related Issues and Biblical Data
A. Reasons for hypocrisy in Bible times

1. Which of the above explanations for hypocrisy apply to those professing to be people of God prior to Christ's life on earth?

Ps. 5:9	Is. 48:1-2	Ezek. 33:30-32
Ps. 55:12-14, 20-23	Is. 65:5	Hos. 10:1, 4
Prov. 26:18-19, 23-26	Is. 66:3-5	Hos. 11:12
Is. 1:13-17	Jer. 7:4, 8-10	Amos 5:21-24
Is. 29:13	Jer. 9:4, 8	Mic. 3:11
Is. 32:7	Jer. 42:20-21	Zech. 7:5-6

2. What explanations did Jesus give for hypocrisy among the Jews?

Mt. 5:20—6:24	Mt. 25:41-45	Lk. 11:37-52
Mt. 7:21-23	Mk. 7:7-8	Lk. 18:11-12
Mt. 21:28-32	Mk. 12:38-40	Jn. 6:26, 70
Mt. 23:2-33	Lk. 6:46	

3. Summarize 1 and 2 by answering the question, Are all who claim to worship one true God genuinely people of God?

4. What are some explanations for hypocrisy in the time of the early church?

Acts 5:1-11	2 Tim. 3:5, 13	1 Jn. 1:6, 10
Rom. 2:1, 3, 17-29	Tit. 1:16	1 Jn. 2:4, 9, 19
Rom. 16:18	Jas. 1:8, 22-24, 26	1 Jn. 4:20
1 Cor. 13:1	Jas. 2:14-26	Jude 12-13
Gal. 2:1-21	2 Pet. 2:1-3, 17, 19	Rev. 2:9
1 Tim. 4:1-2		

5. Summarize this section and answer this question: Are all who claim to be followers of Christ, or hold membership

in Christian churches, truly Christians?

B. The basic root of hypocrisy

1. Why do so many people put on masks?

Jer. 17:9	Mt. 15:7-20	Eph. 2:3
Mt. 7:15-20	Jn. 8:39-44	Eph. 4:18
Mt. 12:33-37	Rom. 7:18	1 Jn. 4:18

2. What is the most basic need a non-Christian has in overcoming hypocrisy?

Jn. 3:1-8	2 Tim. 2:1	1 Pet. 1:22—2:5
2 Cor. 5:17	Tit. 3:1-7	1 Jn. 5:1-5

3. When people are regenerated by the Holy Spirit is their corrupt heart, or "flesh," completely eradicated during this life? When do genuine Christians attain complete Christlikeness?

Rom. 7:14-25	Gal. 5:13-24	1 Jn. 1:5-10
Rom. 8:9-11, 20-23	Phil. 3:12-16	1 Jn. 3:2

4. Since the great power of the Holy Spirit is present with believers, why do they sometimes come so far short of the ideal?

Is. 63:10-19	Eph. 4:30	1 Tim. 4:14
Gal. 3:2-3, 14	1 Thess. 5:19	2 Tim. 1:6

(Consider also the implications of your conclusions on why there is so much suffering in the world, study 3.)

5. Summarize this section by integrating the Bible's teachings on the basic source of hypocritical characteristics.

C. The judgment of hypocrites

1. What factors will God take into account in judging hypocrites?

Mt. 7:1-5, 21-27	Lk. 12:1-3	Rom. 2:1-11, 17-29
Mt. 25:41-45	Lk. 13:10-17	

2. Summarize this section and indicate whether men are best qualified to judge hypocrisy in others or in themselves.

D. Jesus Christ and hypocrisy

1. Considering the reasons for hypocrisy presented in the live options and whatever you know about the life of Christ on earth, answer these questions:

a. Was Christ unrealistic—hating life, cooperation, children and sex?

b. Was he less than honest because of a craving for social acceptance?

c. While professing to be loving, did he lack a visible compassion for others?

d. Did he profess orthodoxy but, in his practical concern for men, deny the realities of a personal God, his enfleshment of deity or the Scriptures as God's faithful word?

e. Was Jesus Christ preoccupied with mere words, substituting them for the realities they designate?

f. Did he profess loyalty to the Father's will and then go his own way?

g. Did he substitute religious rituals for vital experience of the Father?

h. Did Jesus Christ defend the status quo in order to avoid taking any risks in serving others?

i. Did pride and greed combined with the will to power render him the servant not of people but of mere institutional interests?

j. Could it be said that Jesus simply played church, accepting the privileges but refusing the obligations of his faith?

k. Can any evidence be found of Christ bearing the fruit of a corrupt heart or evil nature?

2. Summarize your answers to this section. Can anyone seriously suggest that any pretense of Christian individuals or institutions is to be charged to the Savior himself? Is the sham of many of Christ's alleged followers sufficient reason for rejecting him?

IV. Conclusion

Formulate your answer to the question "Why are there so many hypocrites in the church?" by pulling together your summaries of preceding sections, evaluating the live options (II) with which you differ and interacting with any reading you have done in the sources listed in the notes below.[32]

V. Relevance

A. What applications to contemporary hypocrisy do you see from the role of the elder son in Jesus' parable of the prodigal son (Lk. 15:1-2, 25-32)?

B. Is the charge of hypocrisy more often leveled at Christendom than at many other spheres where it occurs? Why?

C. Is it possible to be moral without being moralistic, ethical without being self-righteous, and religiously critical without pontificating?

D. Evaluate the following quotation from Dietrich Bonhoeffer's *Letters and Papers from Prison:*

There is a kind of malicious satisfaction in knowing that everyone has his weaknesses and nakednesses. In my contacts with the outcasts of society, its pariahs, I have often noticed how mistrust is the dominant motive in their judgments of other people. Every act of a person of high repute, be it ever so altruistic, is suspected from the outset. Incidentally, I find such outcasts in all ranks of society. . . . The less responsible a man's life, the more easily he falls a victim to this attitude.

This irresponsibility and absence of bonds has its counterpart among the clergy in what I should call the "priestly" snuffing around in the sins of men in order to catch them out. It is as if a beautiful house could only be known after a cobweb had been found in the furthermost corner of the cellar, or as though a good play could only be appreciated after one had seen how the actors behave off stage. It is the same kind of thing you find in the novels of the last fifty years, which think they have only depicted their characters properly when they have described them in bed, or in films where it is thought necessary to include undressing scenes. What is clothed, veiled, pure and chaste is considered to be deceitful, disguised and impure, and in fact only shows the impurity of the writers themselves. Mistrust and suspicion as the basic attitude of men is characteristic of the revolt of inferiority.[33]

Notes

[1] A. Maillot, "Falsehood," in *A Companion to the Bible,* ed. J. J. Von Allmen (New York: Oxford University Press, 1958), p. 109.

[2] L. Lemme, "Hypocrisy," in *The Schaff-Herzog Encyclopedia,* ed. Samuel Macauley Jackson (Grand Rapids: Baker Book House, 1953), V, p. 28.

[3] Bertrand Russell, *Why I Am Not a Christian* (New York: Simon and Schuster, 1957), pp. 148-56.

[4] Keith Miller, *The Taste of New Wine* (Waco, Tex.: Word Books, 1965), pp. 21-28.

[5] Francis Schaeffer, *The Church at the End of the 20th Century* (Downers Grove, Ill.: InterVarsity Press, 1970), pp. 71-77, 103-12, 133-53.

[6] Francis Schaeffer, *The Church before the Watching World* (Downers Grove, Ill.: InterVarsity Press, 1971), pp. 52-60.

[7] John A. Mackay, *Christian Reality and Appearance* (Richmond, Va.: John Knox, 1969), pp. 29-30.

[8] Arnold Praeter, *Release from Phoniness* (Waco, Tex.: Word Books, 1968), pp. 33-43.

[9] Mackay, p. 37.

[10] Ibid., p. 66.

[11] Dietrich Bonhoeffer, *Letters and Papers from Prison* (London: Collins, 1953), pp. 164-66.

[12] Deitrich Bonhoeffer, *The Cost of Discipleship* (New York: The Macmillan Company, 1958), p. 38.

[13] Deitrich Bonhoeffer, *Life Together* (New York: Harper and Brothers, 1954), pp. 26-28.

[14] Mackay, p. 84.

[15] Reinhold Niebuhr, *Moral Man and Immoral Society* (New York: Charles Scribner's Sons, 1932), p. 117.

[16] Ibid., p. 141.

[17] James Kavanaugh, *A Modern Priest Looks at His Outdated Church* (New York: Trident Press, 1967), pp. xii, 3.

[18] Edward John Carnell, *The Case for Orthodox Theology* (Philadelphia: The Westminster Press, 1959), p. 121.

[19] Ibid., p. 130, citing H. Richard Niebuhr, *The Social Sources of Denominationalism* (Hamden, Conn.: The Shoestring Press, 1954), p. 11.

[20] Soren Kierkegaard, *Attack Upon Christendom* (Boston: Beacon Press, 1944), p. 8.

[21] Ibid., pp. 32-33, 59.

[22] Ibid., pp. 219-20.

[23] Ibid., pp. 240, 248.

[24] Ibid., pp. 260, 262.

[25] Ibid., pp. 279-80.

[26] Blaise Pascal, *Pensées* (New York: The Modern Library, 1941), No. 100, pp. 40-41.

[27] Ibid., No. 412, p. 130.

[28] Ibid., No. 430, p. 138.

[29] Ibid., No. 453, p. 150.

[30] Ibid., No. 894, p. 314.

[31] Ibid., No. 555, p. 181.

[32] Compare your conclusion here with that of *Decide for Yourself*, study 17.
[33] Bonhoeffer, *Letters and Papers from Prison*, p. 117.

Does Christianity really work personally in today's world?

6

"Why accept Christianity when it has failed in this world for 2,000 years?"

"If God is a God of love, where is the love in the world today?"

"I'm basically content with my life. Why do I need Christ and the Bible?"

"Can Christianity really affect my life more than the sayings of Confucious (or any other way of life)?"

"Does Christianity provide a more meaningful life?"

"Is it possible to 'do my own thing' and have a good time with my peers and still be a Christian?"

"How will being a Christian improve my life?"

I. The Problem

Against the background of extensive hypocrisy, questions understandably arise about the reality of Christian living in this age. Those who ask questions like these are to be commended. Unsatisfied with mere words or institutions, they seek a living reality. If Christian faith is the way to a transforming experience of the God who is there, they want it. If not, they are as well off without it. In order to clarify the actual issues, some observations must be made.

The superficial believism of Christendom, in contrast to faith in the living Christ, does not radically improve one's life. Such a merely nominal Christianity has failed for 2,000 years. Christendom does not exhibit self-sacrificing love in today's world. It lacks the resources to give people the significant sense of identity, purpose and freedom they seek. A kind of "Christianity" which amounts to nothing more than not espousing a non-Christian religion or nothing more than having been born in an allegedly "Christian" country would not merit a study like this.

The question here is whether the responsible commitment of a mature person to the historical Christ as Savior and Lord actually makes a real difference in his manner of existence. A faith which *works* may not necessarily be true. A solely pragmatic test for truth is often unreliable. Contradictory faiths claim this validation. However, a faith which is adequately supported otherwise (that is, logically and factually) must also make a difference in one's way of life. A faith which is true to life works.

Consider also what is meant by *works*. Pragmatists have differed notoriously as to precisely what is necessary to show that a philosophy of life works. We cannot enter into that debate here, but we can suggest that when people ask whether Christianity really works it is necessary for them to identify more specific standards by which they could possibly be satisfied. For the present purposes, we have sought to gather those standards implied in the questions listed on the preceding page. The questioners seem to be asking whether faith in Christ makes life more meaningful, free, authentic (better) and loving. On the ground of these criteria, then, we shall consider whether trusting one's life to the person of Christ works.

II. Live Options

A. According to Bertrand Russell, the English philosopher, Christianity does not work in today's world. Identifying Christianity with mere Christendom, he says a Christian is one who believes in God and immortality and has some belief about Jesus Christ. These beliefs, accepted on emotion not argumentation, warp the natural sympathies, inflict unnecessary suffering, oppose progress and capitalize on fear, and thus lead to cruelty. In short, religious beliefs have made the world unfit to live in. Science is the hope for mankind.[1]

B. Theologies of the future maintain that God makes no difference in the present world but that we are sustained by the hope that he will in the future. God is thought to be totally hidden, eclipsed by something between man and God, or presently "dead." But God will somehow be active in the future. The futurity of God no longer signifies his absence but his presence, his mode of being present as the coming God. So his power in anticipation already qualifies the present. Christianity does not really work in today's world other than in providing a theology of hope.[2]

C. Christianity works here and now, affirms French naturalist Émile Cailliet in his autobiography *Journey into Light.* Cailliet formerly thought life meaningless. His earlier life was described, he said, by James Thomson's "The City of Dreadful Night." "Every struggle brings defeat, ... all the oracles are dumb or cheat, . . . and none can pierce the vast black veil uncertain because there is no light beyond the curtain." Finally, the moment came when Cailliet was overwhelmed with the inadequacy of his views. "Who was I anyway? Nay, what was I? These fundamental questions of human existence remained unanswered." After nine months of hospitalization from war wounds, Cailliet returned to his reading in literature and philosophy in order to find passages that would speak to his condition. But his later reading of his own anthology of choice passages of literature was disappointing. He nearly gave up hope of finding a book that would "understand me, speak to my condition, and help me through life's happenings."

Then he saw a Bible for the first time in his life. As he read the Beatitudes, suddenly the realization dawned upon him: "This was the Book that would understand me!" He found that "its pages were animated by the Presence of the Living God and the power of His mighty acts." As he prayed and read the opening chapters of the Gospel of John, a decisive insight flashed through his whole being. The very clue to the secret of human life was disclosed right there; not stated in the foreboding language of philosophy but in the common, everyday language of human circumstances." He found by experience that response to the Person of the Gospel narrative makes life meaningful. The life of faith, he now testifies, has "only one concern—to do the Lord's will in joy and simplicity of heart." Life for him "is no longer a miserable sequence of broken vows and vain resolutions. It is no longer perpetual effort and struggle or a longing for some extraordinary vision. It is a life of love and power because it is redeemed and fully surrendered life, a life in line with the will of God." The man of power does not give the impression of strain and effort, but what he does God does in him. God's presence produces Christlikeness and issues naturally in worship. Worship because of the power of the Presence is not a mere duty; rather it is "a delectation wherein a Christian's destiny finds its fulfillment."[3]

D. Christ liberates people enslaved by drug addition, John Gimenez testifies from experience. After years of being on drugs, running with gangs and hustling girls, a homeless and hopeless Gimenez met some Christians who cared about him. At first he struggled against the claims of Christ. Finally he turned from his old ways and yielded his life to the Lord. Did it work? "It's like coming home—you can kick off your shoes, and there's a fire burning and a cup of hot tea steaming beside you, and a soothing wife to be there close. This is the kind of thing that happens when I read the Bible. I feel at peace, at ease. The one who has been kicked out by his family, the one who has no place to call his own—he can come home in the Word of God. . . . It's a beautiful thing—a free thing!"

In addition to peace and freedom, he found purpose. "Part of the newness came in wanting to do things—right away I began to work! I'd been on the go all my life, but I never liked work. . . . Now I wanted to do something for God. I wanted to build; I wanted to see things grow. I began to put in plumbing; I began to cook in the kitchen. I was enjoying work for the first time in my life, and I was thirty years old." Many other addicts found Christ through the same community, Brooklyn's Damascus Christian Church. "It isn't a beautiful place by normal standards; yet it's the loveliest place in the world because it's God's factory. It belongs to my Father. And people come—broken people, rotten people, no goods, unwanteds. The misfits of society walk through these open doors to new life."

Because of his faith in Christ, Gimenez found his own life had value and significance. "God, in filling a person with His Holy Spirit is admitting that He needs men. This realization raises a person immediately in his own eyes. Man! You become valuable. It makes you feel important in God's plan. . . . This is the important thing—to be needed." With eight other redeemed addicts, Gimenez now puts on plays dramatizing the way life is before God takes over and the way out of that life. "The first thing we wanted to do with the play was to warn young kids of the awfulness of dope addiction. Then we wanted to let addicts know that they aren't hopelessly twisted forever. We wanted to tell them that Jesus can fill up the empty spaces in their lives and completely change their way of living. We wanted to tell everybody what Jesus Christ has done for us—how He broke the chains of heroin, and made us free."[4]

E. Christian faith contributes to the health of mind and body, according to medical doctor S. I. McMillen. McMillen nearly died from a bleeding ulcer, which he now attributes to overreactions to insignificant matters, such as the constant interruptions of phone messages. Finally, however, he learned to handle stress creatively by applying the principles of Scripture. As God said to the Apostle Paul, "My grace is sufficient for you, for My strength comes to perfection where there is weakness." With Paul, McMillen came to say, "I am happy to take pride rather in my weaknesses, so that the power of Christ may abide in me. I delight, therefore, in weaknesses, in insults, in needy circumstances, in persecutions and dire calamities, all on account of Christ. For when I am weak, then am I strong" (2 Cor. 12:8-10).

In his years of medical experience, he found many patients' conditions worsening in spite of modern medical treatments. Since no capsule could give peace, he wrote a book with a Scriptural prescription for peace, *None of These Diseases*. Replete with case histories and medical statistics, he shows how living according to biblical directives can save a person from certain infectious diseases, many lethal cancers and many psychosomatic illnesses. With psychiatrist William Saddler, he testifies that "a sincere acceptance of the principles and teachings of Christ with respect to the life of mental peace and joy, the life of unselfish thought and clean living would at once wipe out more than half the difficulties, diseases and sorrows of the human race. . . . Laying aside all discussion of the future life, it would pay any man or woman to live the Christ-life just for the mental and moral rewards it affords here in this present world."[5]

F. In the experience of J. B. Phillips, the Bible spoke the truth about reality with contemporary force and relevance. A scholar of the classics at Cambridge for some ten years, he had viewed the New Testament with a "rather snobbish disdain." But as he came to grips with it for his translation *The New Testament in Modern English* he discovered it was not so pedestrian as he supposed. "I found myself," he reported, "provoked, challenged, stimulated, comforted, and generally convicted by my previous shallow knowledge of Scripture." The Bible, he found, "was strangely alive; it spoke to my condition in the most uncanny way. I say 'uncanny' for want of a better word, but it was a very strange experience to sense, not occasionally, but almost continually, the living quality of those rather strangely assorted books. To me it was more remarkable because I had no fundamentalist upbringing. . . . The intervening centuries might never have been; inspired words took on a new, and so to speak, contemporary authority. Indeed, so great was this sense of contemporaneity that we had constantly to remind ourselves of the different conditions of those early days." In contrast to the writings excluded from the New Testament, it included none of the make-believe, myth, magic or fancy. "It was the sustained down-to-earth faith of the New Testament writers which conveyed to me that inexpressible sense of the genuine and the authentic." Trained to distinguish the authentic from the impostor, as experts are in any field, Phillips adds, "It is my serious conclusion that we have in the New Testament, words that bear the hallmark of reality and the ring of truth."[6]

G. Christianity has liberated some primitive Auca tribesmen from fear of demons, vengeance and death and given them the love to risk their lives in reaching others. Dayuma, a frightened Auca girl, fled from her tribe to escape death at the hands of her father's killer. In the Ecuadorian jungle Dayuma met Rachel Saint, sister of one of five missionaries martyred in an earlier attempt to show love to her tribe. Eventually Dayuma responded to the message of God's love and received Christ. Progressively delivered from her fears of vengeance, she convinced other Aucas that the foreigners who loved God came to bring good, not to seek vengeance. Assured of God's love from the words in God's "carving" (the Bible), others became Christians. Contrasting Christian living with their earlier way of life, they said they had learned "to live well."[7]

One of them, Tona, gave his life in an attempt to share the better way with those in the Ridge Auca settlement. Aware of the dangers involved in making this attempt, he may have felt reassured by the fact that his half-brother Wepe was among them. Later it was learned, however, that when Tona came, Wepe said, "He is another, or outsider, not my brother as he claims to be," and invited the people to spear him. Tona's death has not caused the Christian Aucas to plan a killing expedition, as it would have twenty years ago. Instead, exchange visits have been arranged, an airstrip built at the Ridge settlement and other steps taken to evangelize them. The missionaries and the Aucas, who have both risked and sacrificed their lives for the sake of others, have demonstrated the self-giving love of their Savior.[8]

H. The walk of faith has given Francis and Edith Schaeffer a highly fulfilling life of loving service. Leaving the security of a fine pastorate in America, they and their children journeyed to a Europe still deeply scarred by the Second World War. In spite of many unknowns, including illness and legal testings, they established a "shelter" for disillusioned people seeking reality. L'Abri (the shelter) stands today as a symbol of God's power to lead and provide for those who will walk a step at a time by faith.

As Edith Schaeffer acknowledges, "Jumping from one change to another, from one big answer to prayer to another, from one surprise development to another, may give a false impression. . . . It has not been an exciting succession of 'success.' There have been sicknesses, accidents, depressions, discouragement, frustrations and exhaustion. There has been a succession of temptations to give up, to call it too much, to say we have had enough and that we want to have a 'normal life like other people.' There have been what we feel sure are direct attacks of Satan to stop us, to make us give up. . . . To say the least, . . . it is far from a soft life. But there is *reality*. There is certainty of the God who is there. There is the possibility of seeing that God works in space, time and history, and in one's own moment of history. There is the certainty of being in communication with Him rather than having some nebulous psychological crutch to enable one to bear life."[9]

Through the ministry of L'Abri many other lives have been given meaning. "Professors, pastors, doctors, lawyers, artists, architects, writers, musicians, nurses, schoolteachers, secretaries, scientists, actors, students of all kinds and varieties—as well as drop-outs and opt-outs! There were Japanese studying in Germany, French, Italians, Germans, Dutch, English, Scots, Irish, Canadians, Americans from many different states, Swiss, South Americans, Scandinavians, Australians, New Zealanders and South Africans. There were long haired boys, and a wide variety of beards and dress; long haired girls, the beatniky types and the ultra-fashionable types. . . . Every sort of religious and philosophic background seemed to be represented with a twentieth century unification among them, in an inability to believe that truth exists—yet with a hunger to find meaning, not being satisfied with the 'plastic universe' of today."[10]

III. Debated Issues and Biblical Data

The primary focus of this study is Christianity's relevance for an individual's life. In our quest for relevance, however, we must not lose sight of genuine Christianity. The most responsible way in which to speak of *Christianity's* relevance is in terms of its most authentic sources, its primary sources, the Scriptures. In investigating the present significance of the Scriptures, we should keep before us such questions as: What resources do people utilize who find Christianity to work in their experience? Or, If Christianity works today as it did in Bible times, what will it do for us?

A. Personal identity and a meaningful life

1. As a Christian asks "Who am I?" what aspects of his identity does he share with all other human beings (Christian and non-Christian)?

Gen. 5:1-2   Mk. 7:21-23   Rom. 3:10, 23

2. What aspects of the Christian's identity are shared with all other believers in Jesus Christ?

1 Cor. 6:17-21   Eph. 1:4-7   Eph. 3:7-11
1 Cor. 12:4-7

3. How does a Christian have uniqueness as an individual?[11]

1 Cor. 12:8-27

4. To what does a Christian owe his identity as a person gifted to build up the church?

1 Cor. 15:10   Eph. 3:7-8

5. Of how much value is each human person?

Mt. 10:29-31   Mk. 8:34-37   1 Pet. 3:3-4
Mt. 18:1-14   Jn. 12:24-25

6. Does paying attention to the Bible make life more meaningful?[12]

Ps. 19:7-11   Ps. 119:93, 105, 165   2 Tim. 3:15-17
Ps. 119:9, 45, 63

7. What goals give purpose to a Christian's life here and now?

Jn. 17:17-19   1 Cor. 10:31   Eph. 4:13
Jn. 18:37   1 Cor. 12:31   Phil. 3:13-14
1 Cor. 6:20   1 Cor. 14:12   Heb. 6:1

8. Summarize this section by answering the question, Does Christianity provide a meaningful life in today's world?

B. Freedom to be yourself

1. Is a Christian forced into having new life, or is he attracted to it by love?

Jer. 31:3   Jn. 3:16   1 Jn. 4:19

Hos. 11:4   Rom. 5:8

2. What response above all others does God desire man to express freely?

Mt. 22:36-40   Col. 3:14   1 Pet. 4:8

3. Evaluate the following summation of Augustine's concept of freedom and its relation to love (in terms of the verses listed under questions B1 and B2).

The most valuable freedom is not the psychological freedom to do what we will, not the physical, social or political freedom which exempts us from illegitimate interference from others, not the Stoic freedom of following the law of nature nor the Kantian freedom of doing what we ought, but the Divine freedom . . . of wanting to do what we ought because we love God and take delight in Him. . . .

If one's love is whole, one's will is whole; when one's will is whole the person is unified; when one's love is good, the person is good. . . . By servitude to God man obtains self-mastery. The knowledge that freedom is a matter of "cleaving to God" is one thing; the cleaving itself is another. . . . The sign of victory is harmony. Harmony in man is . . . only attained by a love great enough to embrace all loves. . . . Liberty as the love of God . . . will distinguish the citizens of God's city from those of the earthly city of self-love. . . .

Efficacious grace is victorious without being constraining. . . . It is a grace that does not cause us to act but causes us to want to act . . . it substitutes delight in the good for delight in evil. Man is not constrained to keep a law previously repugnant to him, but he spontaneously finds his joy in it. . . .

Augustine had discovered that the key to human freedom and fulfillment is right love and had announced as a program for freedom: Love God and do as you please. . . . Only when a person wants to be what he should be is he fulfilled as a person and consequently happy. . . . We are not slaves because we obey rules, nor are we free because we disregard them. Not the rules as such but our relation to them determines whether in obeying or disobeying we are free or slaves. . . . The principal feature of the will is not its independence but its love, a joyous assent to all reality and perfection.[13]

4. Why do some people not trust Christ and find freedom in his truth?

Jn. 3:19   Jn. 8:42   Jn. 14:24

5. Is a Christian free to think and say what he happens to like at a given time, or must he think and say what is true about reality?

Jn. 8:31-36

6. From what types of tyrannies is the Christian liberated?

Jn. 8:34   Gal. 4:3, 8-9, 21-31   1 Pet. 2:16
Rom. 6:12-19   Gal. 5:13   2 Pet. 2:19

7. Is a person most free when acting in the "flesh" contrary to the Spirit or when filled with the Holy Spirit?

Jn. 8:34-36   Rom. 8:7, 15   2 Cor. 3:17
Acts 4:8-13, 31

8. What are the characteristics of a life liberated by Christ and the Holy Spirit?

Rom. 8:16   Gal. 5:22-23   Heb. 2:14-15
Gal. 4:6   Eph. 4—6   Heb. 13:5
Gal. 5:6   Col. 3—4   1 Jn. 4:7

9. How free is a person when his will is divided between two ultimate allegiances?

Mt. 6:24   Mt. 13:44-46   Jas. 1:6-8
Mt. 10:37-39   Jn. 12:25   Jas. 4:8

10. Describe the experience of a person who is free to choose a goal but not to achieve it.

Rom. 7:15-25

11. How did obedience to God set Peter free?

Acts 5:27-32   Acts 10:28, 34-43   Acts 11:1-18

12. What freedoms did Paul enjoy through Christ?

Phil. 3:2-21   Phil. 4:11-13, 19

13. Summarize this section by answering the question, To what extent is a Christian free to be himself, to "do his own thing"?

C. Openness and integrity

1. Describe what happens when people take off their masks and face up to their real, sinful condition.

Ps. 32:3-7   Ps. 139:1-12   1 Jn. 1:9

Ps. 51:1-12   Jas. 5:16

2. On what grounds can a Christian accept and believe in his own potential? In addition to being created in God's likeness, redeemed and given spiritual gifts, what other advantages does he have?

Ps. 29:11   Is. 40:29   Jn. 15:15-16

Ps. 32:8   Dan. 11:32

3. How can a Christian reassure himself when his heart condemns him?

Heb. 9:9, 14   Heb. 10:21-22   1 Jn. 3:18-22

4. What attitudes does a mature Christian have toward those with weak consciences?

1 Cor. 8:7-13   1 Cor. 10:23—11:1

5. What may happen to the conscience of one who accepts the ideas of deceitful spirits and pretentious liars?

1 Tim. 4:1-2   Tit. 1:15-16

6. In what way must church leaders be honest about their faith?[14]

1 Tim. 3:9

7. How may a Christian's objectives regarding personal authenticity be expressed?

2 Cor. 1:12   Phil. 4:8   Heb. 13:18

2 Cor. 4:2   1 Thess. 4:11-12   Jas. 3:17-18

2 Cor. 8:21   1 Tim. 1:5, 19   1 Pet. 3:16

8. In what terms did Paul describe his own integrity?

Acts 23:1 Rom. 9:1 2 Tim. 1:3

Acts 24:16

9. Are any limits placed on a Christian's openness and honesty?

1 Cor. 3:21-23 Eph. 4:15, 25-32

10. Summarize this section by answering the question, How can being a Christian improve my life?

D. Existing in love

1. On what basis can fallen people rely on God's acceptance and understanding?

Eph. 1:6-10 Eph. 3:12 Heb. 4:14-16

Eph. 2:12-13

2. On what bases may Christians and non-Christians accept each other?

Acts 17:26 Jas. 3:9-10 Jas. 5:7-11

Jas. 2:8-26 Jas. 4:11-12

3. For what other reasons can a Christian enjoy loving acceptance from other Christians?

1 Jn. 2:9-11 1 Jn. 4:7-12 1 Jn. 4:20—5:1

1 Jn. 3:11-18

4. Evaluate Deitrich Bonhoeffer's view of love for others. Does he make good a distinction between Christian love and a merely humanistic love?

Human love is directed to the other person for his own sake, spiritual love loves him for Christ's sake. . . . [It] loves him not as a free person but as one whom it binds to itself. It wants to gain, to capture by every means; it uses force. It desires to be irresistible, to rule. Human love has little regard for truth. It makes the truth relative, since nothing, not even the truth, must come between it and the beloved person . . . human love cannot love an enemy, that is, one who seriously and stubbornly resists it. . . . Human love makes itself an end in itself . . . an idol which it worships, to which it must subject everything. . . . Spiritual love, however, comes from Jesus Christ, it serves him alone; it knows that it has no immediate access to other persons. Jesus Christ stands between the lover and the others he loves. I do not know in advance what love of others means . . . only Christ tells in His Word. . . . Spiritual love is bound solely by the Word of Jesus Christ. Where Christ bids me to maintain fellowship for the sake of love, I will maintain it. Where his truth enjoins me to dissolve a fellowship for love's sake, there I will dissolve it, despite all the protests of my human love. Because spiritual love does not desire but rather serves, it loves an enemy as a brother . . . it is something strange, new and incomprehensible to all earthly love. . . . I must release the other person from every attempt of mine to regulate, coerce, and dominate him with my love. The other person needs to retain his independence of me; to be loved for what he is, as one for whom Christ became man, died and rose again, for whom Christ bought forgiveness of sins and eternal life. Because Christ has long since acted decisively for my brother, before I could begin to act, I must leave him his freedom to be Christ's; I must meet him only as the person that he already is in Christ's eyes. . . . Human love constructs its own image of the other person, of what he is and what he should become. It takes the life of the other person into its own hands . . . spiritual love creates *freedom* of the brethren under the Word.[15]

5. What does Christian love do for the one who loves?

Col. 3:14   1 Jn. 4:16-18

6. What does Christian love do for the ones who are loved?

Jn. 15:13   1 Cor. 8:1   1 Pet. 4:8-9
Rom. 13:8-10   1 Cor. 13:1-8

7. What types of people are Christians to love?

Mt. 5:43-48   Lk. 10:30-37   Rom. 13:9
Mt. 25:34-40   Jn. 13:34-35   1 Jn. 4:11, 20-21

8. In what ways do the central figures in the following passages exhibit their inner love?

Lk. 7:36-50   Lk. 15:11-32   2 Cor. 2:4
Lk. 10:30-37   Acts 9:36, 39   1 Thess. 2:8

9. What dynamic makes love workable today?

Jn. 13:34   Rom. 5:5   Gal. 5:22
Jn. 14:12-31   2 Cor. 5:14   1 Jn. 4:19

10. Summarize this section by answering the question, Where is love in the world today?

IV. Conclusion

Formulate your answer to the question "Does Christianity really work personally in today's world?" by pulling together your summaries of the preceding sections, evaluating the live options (II) with which you differ, interacting with any reading you have done in the sources listed in the notes below, and interpreting your own experience and that of other Christians.

V. Relevance

A. If people were to observe your life for a few weeks, would they see Christianity working for you? In what ways would you exhibit the dynamics of Christian faith?

B. According to the following testimony, how did Christianity work for Blaise Pascal?

I love poverty because He loved it. I love riches because they afford me the means of helping the very poor. I keep faith with everybody; I do not render evil to those who wrong me, but I wish them a lot like mine, in which I receive neither evil nor good from men. I try to be just, true, sincere, and faithful to all men; I have a tender heart for those to whom God has more closely united me; and whether I am alone, or seen of men, I do all my actions in the sight of God, who must judge of them, and to whom I have consecrated them all.

These are my sentiments; and every day of my life I bless my Redeemer, who has implanted them in me, and who, of a man full of weakness, of miseries, of lust, of pride, and of ambition, has made a man free from all these evils by the power of His grace, to which all the glory of it is due, as of myself I have only misery and error.[16]

Notes

[1] Bertrand Russell, *Why I Am Not a Christian* (New York: Simon and Schuster, 1957), pp. 3-23.
[2] For a clear survey of theologies of the future, see Peter C. Hodgson, *Jesus–Word and Presence: An Essay in Christology* (Philadelphia: Fortress Press, 1971), pp. 2-27.
[3] Émile Cailliet, *Journey into Light* (Grand Rapids: Zondervan, 1968), pp. 11-18, 98, 105-06.
[4] John Gimenez with Char Meredith, *Up Tight* (Waco, Tex.: Word Books, 1967), pp. 70-76.
[5] S. I. McMillen, *None of These Diseases* (Old Tappen, N.J.: Fleming H. Revell, 1963), pp. 7-8, 111.
[6] J. B. Phillips, *Ring of Truth: A Translator's Testimony* (New York: The Macmillan Company, 1967), pp. 24-26, 124-25.
[7] Ethel Emily Wallis, *The Dayuma Story: Life Under Auca Spears* (New York: Harper and Brothers, 1960), p. 204.
[8] Joseph T. Bayly, "The Latest Auca Martyr," *Eternity*, January 1972, pp. 47-48.
[9] Edith Schaeffer, *L'Abri* (Wheaton, Ill.: Tyndale House, 1969), p. 226.
[10] Ibid., p. 210.
[11] See also Robert James St. Clair, *The Adventure of Being You* (Westwood, N.J.: Fleming H. Revell, 1966), pp. 1-181.
[12] For further reading, see David A. Hubbard, *Does the Bible Really Work?* (Waco, Tex.: Word Books, 1971), pp. 33-38, 51-57, 64-70.
[13] Mary T. Clark, *Augustine: Philosopher of Freedom* (New York: Desclee, 1958), pp. 69, 74, 76, 79, 103-05, 175, 178, 213 and 246; for further reading see Michael Green, *Jesus Spells Freedom* (Downers Grove, Ill.: InterVarsity Press, 1972), pp. 1-128.
[14] Elton Trueblood, "Intellectual Integrity," in *The New Man for Our Time* (New York: Harper and Row, 1970), pp. 105-26.
[15] Dietrich Bonhoeffer, *Life Together* (New York: Harper and Brothers, 1954), pp. 34-37.
[16] Relate your conclusion to that of *Decide for Yourself*, study 18.
[17] Blaise Pascal, *Pensées* (New York: The Modern Library, 1941), p. 174.

Does a Christian's faith really work in his relationships with others?

7

"Can Christ really make the world a better place?"

"How can a book as old as the Bible be relevant?"

"What good has the church done in the world?"

"How is Christianity relevant to war, poverty and racism?"

"Isn't Christianity just a list of do's and don't's? What does it provide here and now?"

"How can a just God condone war?"

"What about population control, and questions related to the value of life?"

"When God said man was to have dominion over the earth, didn't that lead to exploitation of it?"

"Isn't Christianity opposed to ecological balance?"

"How are you Christians involved in correcting social problems like pollution, violence and racism?"

"Didn't Christ preach revolutionary social relations and a new life style rather than some far-off kingdom?"

"Christianity is essentially conservative, isn't it? We've tried that, haven't we?"

I. The Problem

Even if a person grants that trust in Christ helps individuals find identity, freedom, integrity and love, questions persist concerning the outworking of the Christian faith in crucial areas of human societal existence today. People who care about other human beings are asking questions like those on the preceding page.

As in the previous study, *Christianity* is here understood to designate a personally experienced, biblically revealed faith in the living Christ. In the questions above, the criteria for its "working" in relationships among people center upon its dealing with poverty, race, war and pollution. This study investigates the resources Christians have for facing these problems and the involvement Christians have in meeting these urgent needs.

An informed biblical faith does not promise instant utopia. Easy answers to difficult problems are not available for two major reasons. First, Christ's kingdom, with its social and political perfection, awaits his return to the earth. Only when the Prince of Peace rules universally in unveiled holy love and all-wise power will social problems that now exist be completely alleviated. Second, there is a great gap between any man's ideals and his behavior. This is true for Christians as well as non-Christians; in fact, it confirms the doctrine of man's sinful nature. Christianity's claim is that salvation makes possible not a total release from selfishness, greed, prejudice and brutality, but a substantial, progressive deliverance from their power throughout this life. The problem of this study, then, is to determine whether such a significant difference is in fact experienced in the present troubled times.

II. Live Options

A. The traditional Christian faith and the Christian church do not improve human relations, according to Pierre Berton in his scathing denunciation, *The Comfortable Pew.* The institutional church, he argues, is of so little value to the needy masses of people today that it should be destroyed. He would ban sermons, scrap pulpits, abandon the familiar concept of God the Father, throw out the Bible stories, do away with religion and tear down the churches, or at least relegate them to the side streets. If Berton were to have his way, what would be left? "Christian love, in all its flexibility, with all of its concern for real people rather than for any fixed set of rigid principles."[1]

Why did Berton launch this revolutionary attack on the established church (in this case the Anglican Church of Canada)? Church members, he found, rationalized a lack of Christlike compassion and action on the selfish basis of preserving their church's program and unity. They did not worship God so much as conformity and respectability. In business practices the great commandment of the twentieth century has been "Thou shalt covet." With few exceptions the church upheld every government decision concerning war and killing. It has been a force for preserving the status quo, suppressing any conscious protest of present policy. Contrary to the example of Christ, who traveled with the outcasts of society, the contemporary church is success-oriented. Although Christianity started as a revolutionary religion, it has become nothing more than a useful tool for winning wars and hockey games or gaining an advantage in the business world. Rather than trying to reform the church, Berton left the church. In his judgment it was hopelessly irrecoverable as a force for effective action against greed, injustice, prejudice and poverty.[2]

B. Faith in Christ enabled Frank Laubach to help thousands of poor people help themselves. For fifteen years this missionary's attempts to break through the barriers of the

Moros in Lanao province of the Philippine Islands had failed. At the end of himself, Laubach finally realized he did not really love these filthy betel nut chewers, these theives and murderers. He felt superior, but also guilty for his failure. In agony he cried out, "Lord, come and change me. Make me over!" He came to realize that more important than what he *did* was what he *was*. With a new love in his heart, he again passed the Muslim priests, who had the usual hatred in their eyes, but this time Laubach said, "I want to study your Koran. Will you teach me?" With communication barriers broken down, he reduced their language to writing and in a short time developed an excellent method for teaching people how to read. He trained twenty teachers, who in turn taught hundreds more to read. Their previous animosity melted away, and within a year most of the people in the province had become his friends.

When mission funds were seriously cut back, the teachers could not be supported and the literacy campaign had to stop. The tribesmen, most armed with knives and guns, confronted Laubach sternly. Finally a chief said, "I'll make everybody who knows how to read teach somebody else—or I'll kill him!" The slogan then was "Teach or die." Dr. Laubach changed the slogan to "Each one teach one." What could be better for a newly literate person than to share his skill with someone else? It became clear that this was the key to the problem of literacy around the world. If the world's illiterates had to wait for highly trained teachers and specially constructed schools, many would wait in vain. In a remarkably short time, 70,000 Moros became literate. Then Laubach was asked to adapt his method to other Philippine languages and soon had invitations from all over the world. He traveled from country to country and lived to see his program in effect in approximately three hundred languages in a hundred different countries. It is estimated that almost 100 million people learned to read through this program.

A devout man, Frank Laubach sought to live constantly in

God's presence. In his diary he wrote, "Everything worth doing flowed from these hours when I was in contact with God. Every wasted hour was when I forgot Him." Prayer for people was important, but not enough. "If we pray only," he said, "we soon cease to do even that." He sought a balance between prayer and service. With all that he did, his greatest joy came from witnessing to others about the Savior. "As you are instructing the illiterate, love him and pray for him. Treat him as your friend. Then one day when he looks up at you and asks, 'Why are you doing all this? Why do you spend so much time and effort on me?' you can smile and say to him, 'I'm doing it because Christ loves you. He is the best friend a man ever had.' " To Dr. Laubach it was unthinkable that a Christian could spend time with anyone without referring to the love of Christ and his offer of abundant life. A great scholar, Laubach earned six academic degrees, authored over thirty-five books and was acclaimed by the leaders of governments around the world. Yet the greenest student felt at ease in his presence. Millions from New Mexico to New Guinea are grateful that such a man lived and through Christ learned to love and serve.[3]

C. Sociologist David O. Moberg has found that social problems, in the final analysis, are intensely personal problems for their victims. In such human dilemmas, Christianity provides "moral guidance in the name of God." Christianity's realism is confirmed as sociology "demonstrates that there is always a gap between the ideal and the real . . . that men are sinful. . . . The rebellious failure of men who classify themselves as righteous to see their own unrighteousness— only that of their enemies or even their brothers—lies behind many of the problems of churches, individuals and society." In such situations, the principles provided by divine revelation enable one to transcend personal biases and economic blind spots and give a prime foundation for responsible criticism of things like hypocritical tokenism in government and other institutions. Christianity also provides positive proposals for actions to be taken. "Witch hunting crusades may divert Christians from their primary mission. God's positive will for society will not be proclaimed when the church spends most of her energy combating . . . real or imagined enemies. The way to overcome evil is to do good (Rom. 12:14-21)."

Because of his Christian convictions, Moberg has confidence that "even the most unpromising derelict, from the human perspective, can be redeemed by God's grace. As God forgives the vilest sinners who call upon Him, we must be ready to forgive those who need to make a new start in life." Christianity, in the face of a conflict between property rights and human rights, gives precedence to human rights. Moberg cites instances in which churches have been revitalized by showing that they exist to serve rather than to be served. People see little reason for paying any attention to a church that never pays attention to them. Churches which have become concerned for the living needs of families around them have reversed a gradual decline in membership and begun to grow. A Christian system of values, Moberg finds, can be tested in certain aspects through sociological research methods. Theology not only provides many interesting hypotheses for empirical testing but also sensitizes sociologists to issues often overlooked in their analyses of social phenomena.

Does this noted authority identify Christianity with a passé traditionalism? "The Christian is a conservative who tries to conserve all that is true, honest, just, pure, lovely, and gracious (Phil. 4:8) in society and a liberal who tries to liberate mankind by changing conditions of society that violate those criteria of excellence. It is dangerous to change for the sake of change alone, and equally dangerous to support the status quo just because 'we've always done it this way.' " He further explains, "Christians should test all relevant evidence carefully and then hold fast what is good, abstaining from that which appears to be evil (1 Thess. 5:21-22). They should distinguish between fact and opinion, between Bible teachings and interpretations of the Bible, between wholesome conservatism and obstructionist traditionalism, and between healthy modification of the current situation and revolutionary revision that would destroy good elements of the present social order along with the bad."[4]

D. Has Christianity worked for Africans? Jackson O. Amobonye, Civil Servant in Nigeria, answers that question in an interview, "Western Civilization, a Curse or a Blessing?" He says, "In my opinion, Western civilization has contributed immensely to the development of Africa, thus acting as a blessing. Education came with Western civilization to Africa. Especially in our country, Nigeria, education has been the source of wealth and has created immense improvement in many societies. Through education we are able to have many judges and lawyers in the country. Politics is a product of Western civilization and it is achieved through education. Western civilization enables us to know our rights; every citizen knows that it is his duty to obey the law. The system of the modern way of marriage—monogamy—is one of the blessings we inherited from Western civilization. During the era of our forefathers, they lived polygamous lives, and this created more family trouble and disaster during their lifetime. But since we have responded to the call of Western civilization which bids us to monogamy, things proceed smoothly and lovers (husband and wife) find it easy to share their love with one another. Religion is not an exception; the introduction of Christianity began with Western civilization. This religion has made abundant contributions to the development of Africa. The abolition of slavery and slave trade by the humanitarians was brought about through Christianity. Human sacrifices of the olden days had ceased to prevail; the spirit of wickedness and atrocity faded away and the new spirit of love is attained. . . . Socialism, . . . the art of living together happily in a community, has come through Western civilization. By uniting ourselves with others, we are able to learn etiquette; thus a social person is mannerly and finds himself fitted for companionship. If we really examine our everyday living, we shall certainly be convinced that Western civilization is a great blessing to us."[5]

E. Christianity has worked significantly for Tom Skinner, a former Harlem gang leader. In an extensive chapter on "The Workability of the Gospel" in *How Black Is the Gospel?* he shows how his faith solved the problems of identity, community and power. "If you ask 'Tom, how does that work, how can it become relevant to my personal life, how can I be sure all you say that the gospel is, theoretically can be applied to our everyday lives?' The way that I must answer is, to say it worked practically through my own life.

"I have not had to negate my blackness in order to be a Christian, but rather, now that I am committed to Jesus Christ, it is God's desire to live His life through my 'redeemed blackness.' I'm God's son; I am a member of a royal family of God, which puts me in the best family stock there is in all the world, which makes me better off than the Queen of England's kids and the kids of the president of the United States. . . . Black is beautiful, but a lot more than that, a lot more beautiful, since Jesus Christ is living through it, and one of the things I have discovered is that Jesus looks great in black.

"I don't have to hate my white friend in order to prove to him that I am secure. Neither do I have to change his attitude toward me. . . . I know who I am, whether others know it or not. Therefore, I can simply be myself. This does not mean that I am not committed to justice, to the black man's struggle, to the black revolution, because I am. Anybody who has observed the social scene, anybody who knows what's going on, knows that the black revolution—in the sense of seeking to obtain economic, social and political power, rectify injustices, eliminate poverty and exploitation of people in the black community—is a just cause. The difference is that I no longer go out and fight for dignity for myself because I already have it, as God's son. I am now engaged in a fight against injustice, a fight against social inequality. But as God's son, I've got to obey God's Word.... So I become involved in boycotting the chain store in my neighborhood which is charging 25 percent more for food than is charged in the white community just south of me, because that is unjust, and the justice of the kingdom of God, to which I belong, demands that I do something about it. I become involved in rent strikes.... I am involved in trying to get the schools in my community decentralized ... not because I am out for anything personal; I am out to rectify injustice—be it black or white—as a member of the Kingdom of God. The difference is that, as God's son, my fight must be based on the principles of the Kingdom of God. I do not have to hate my white brother or my white friends while demanding justice. I do not have to be at the point where I want to kill him. In other words, I am willing to go out and fight, willing to give my life to rectify unjust causes, but I am not going to become unjust myself in the process. Because I am God's son.

"Secondly, not only do I know who I am, I know what I've got. The Bible tells me that I am not only God's son but also a joint heir with Jesus Christ.... 'All the love that it takes to be a man, all the patience that it takes to be a man, all the mercy and all the joy and all the temperance that it takes to be a man, is mine in this person of Jesus Christ.... I have a sense of security, not only as to who I am but what I have, a sense that God guides my destiny, that I belong to Him, that my now and my future is His. Therefore, I can deal with my brother. I can deal with my black brother and my white brother with a sense of security.'

"And three, the Bible tells me, in the book of Ephesians, that I am seated together with Jesus Christ in the heavenly places, which puts me on the highest social level in all the world. I swing with Jesus Christ and company. I don't have to break my neck to belong to any particular social group, because I am already on the highest social level.

"My attitude toward my neighbor is: Because Jesus Christ is alive in me, all I ask is to love you. Whether you love me back or not is unimportant. I can now derive enough love from the life of Jesus Christ to be able to survive without your love. But what I do ask for is the privilege of loving you.

"But just because I love him (my white neighbor) does not mean I will allow him to walk all over me; it does not mean that I will not stand against his injustice; it does not mean that I will not fight him at the point of inequality. But in doing so, I will do it with love and compassion and always in an attempt to reconcile him to me and to my Savior.

"I now have the power to pull it off. In me there is the living Christ; in me is the very power of God Himself. . . . In other words, for everything that God asks me to do, for every demand that God makes upon me, for every command He gives me, He is available in me to turn around and do it through me. This makes Jesus Christ exciting! This makes the Christian life vibrant!

"So I have solved the problem of identity, the problem of community, and the problem of power. The gospel of Jesus Christ is relevant to the black man's condition. It is relevant in liberating that man. It is relevant in showing him what his responsibility is."[6]

F. Does Christianity help a politician as he faces the complex issues of a nation in the midst of pressures from many diverse groups? According to John B. Anderson, a leader in the United States House of Representatives, it does. Converted to Christ as a boy in Rockford, Illinois, Anderson now serves on the influential Rules Committee determining which bills will come before the House for consideration and decision. In the inflammatory sixties, one of the most hotly debated issues was the Federal Open Housing Statute. The Rules Committee made its decision in 1968 on the day Martin Luther King was buried. Anderson cast the deciding vote in an 8 to 7 decision, voting against other members of his own party. His speech in support of equal housing opportunities for all races received an overwhelming response, and two days later President Johnson signed into law the Civil Rights Act of 1968.

How does Christianity contribute to Anderson's life of decision-making in the midst of such pressures? "Dedicated Christians can disagree, and disagree widely, on particular political questions. . . . But faith can play a vital role in the decision-making process. Often I have occasion to resort to prayer, . . . my own worship experience has often been an important part of the process. . . . On many occasions as I have attended a Sunday morning service . . . I have been deeply moved by the thought that the Pastor and the congregation were upholding us in prayer. I can also think of sermons that have brought home a spiritual truth with great impact, and have given me a clearer insight into some of the problems that we deal with in Congress. Personal Bible study is also important to me. There isn't a book that is more influential in my life, or more important in giving me a sense of the Divine purpose that rules all of our lives. This Scripture reading keeps forcefully before me the fact that God does care about what we think and what we do, and how we do it. . . . The counsel of other Christians can also be helpful. During the debate over the open housing bill in the spring of 1968, talks with some of my Christian friends gave me a great feeling of their depth of concern for this problem, and Christian compassion as revealed in these conversations certainly played a part in the ultimate decision that I made. . . . Is it actually possible to chart a course compatible with personal Christian faith, and to be true to one's convictions despite these pressures (from people, groups, party members, etc.)? My answer is short, and I hope not deceptively simple: God can give us, through His grace and power, the wisdom and strength that we lack in and of ourselves. . . . I pray daily for real wisdom and understanding, to be able to surmount some of these pressures. . . . My overriding conviction is that faith and trust in the power of God can aid me in any situation.

"The attempted legitimization of violence is based on the belief that our institutions, both public and private, have lost any right to continue to exist because they are part of a system that simply does not work. . . . The spiritual progenitor of many of these modern revolutionaries is Mao Tse Tung, who teaches that power grows out of a gun barrel. . . . I believe that the motive force behind genuine progress is not the power that grows out of a gun barrel, but the power of the idea that man is a spiritual being. It follows that only as we maximize the opportunities for expression of spirit, in a climate free of oppression and discrimination, will we move toward the goal of allowing everyone to achieve his full potential. The Scriptures tell us that 'where the Spirit of the Lord is, there is liberty.' If we, as Christians, are truly filled with the Spirit, we will seek to do those things that will enlarge the freedom of all our fellow men.

"If our love is broad enough to extend to our neighbor's child, we will be willing to support those actions that will assure him equal educational opportunity. But first we must be willing to look at the problem with a Christian conscience, and in a spirit that says, 'I will judge this issue with a heart that is ruled, not by prejudice or hatred, but by the same love that Christ showed toward me.' We can only hope to bridge the awful gap that has opened between black and white in our society with the instrumentality of Christian love.

"Believing as I do that Christ's words to Nicodemus are relevant to the situation of modern man, and that we must be born again, in no way relieves me of my responsibility to pursue social justice, to act in compassion toward my fellow men, and to seek a better world. For, while man is a sinner, God has implanted within each of us a conscience, and with it we become responsible for our own actions and chargeable with the responsibility to do mercy, seek justice and walk humbly before our God."[7]

G. Christian convictions, as Jacques Ellul understands them, forbid participation in all war and violence, even to help the poor. This professor of law and government at the University of Bordeaux, France, argues that violence begets only more violence and nothing else—no matter how much propaganda is used to rationalize it. In accepting the authority of Christ, Christians must "reject violence, root and branch." To use violence is to be of the world.

What then is the Christian to do in the face of injustice? "The main duty of the Christian nowadays is to urge the cause of the oppressed pacifically, to witness to their misery and to call for justice. The Christian should serve as an intermediary or mediator between the powerful and the oppressed. He is the spokesman appointed by God for the oppressed. This role is much more difficult and thankless than that of a guerrilla chieftain or a corporation head. To gain entrance to a corporation head and insist on discussing his workers' plight with him is much more difficult than to march in a picket line, for it requires much more in the way of intelligence, ability, precise information, and strength of soul. . . . The Christian has spiritual weapons. . . . But some will say this is utopian! No. It is an expression of faith. And if we do not believe that the Lord in whom we trust can open the mouth of the dumb and move mountains, we have simply abandoned Christianity completely. . . . Once violence is there, it is too late. And then Christians cannot try to redeem themselves and soothe their consciences by participating in violence. . . . It is the heart of the problem that must be attacked. And Christians alone can do that—because the others know nothing about all this, and because only the Christians receive the power of the Holy Spirit and are required by God to do these things. . . . Spiritual warfare is just as brutal as human warfare. We know what price Jesus paid for waging his battle spiritually. . . . We are to wage the warfare of faith, our only weapons those Paul speaks of: prayer, the Word of God, the justice of God, the zeal with which the gospel of peace endows us, the sword of the Spirit. And if we think this is easy, it is because we know nothing about life in Christ, because we are so sunk in our materialistic culture that we have quite forgotten the meaning of God's work in us, quite forgotten what we are called to in the world."[8]

H. Christianity also has something significant to offer to meet the ecological crisis of our globe, according to Francis Schaeffer in *Pollution and the Death of Man: The Christian View of Ecology*. The Christian view of man and nature differs from pantheism, which reduces man's personality and dignity and leaves him with de Sade's dictum, "What is, is right," in morals, and man is nothing more than grass. Christianity also differs from Platonic religions, which, in fixing their gaze upon heaven, may lead men to be unkind to animals and to live in ugly surroundings.

According to Christianity, everything in nature has value because God made it. Schaeffer seeks to treat each thing with integrity because that is the way God made it. The value of each is not in itself autonomously, but in the order God intended. Schaeffer honors what God has made "up to the very highest level that he can honor it, without sacrificing man." Because of his Christian philosophy, he does not destroy trees, birds or animals without reason.

Man's fall into sin not only separated him from God and other men but also from nature (which itself was cursed). Eventually, nature, which has been subject to bondage until now, will be totally redeemed. "The Christian who believes the Bible should be the man who—with God's help in the power of the Holy Spirit—is treating nature now in the direction of the way nature will be then. It will not now be perfect, but it must be substantial, or we have missed our calling. God's calling to the Christian now, and to the Christian community, in the area of nature—just as in the area of personal Christian living in true spirituality—is that we should exhibit a substantial healing here and now, between man and nature and nature and itself, as far as Christians can bring it to pass."

Each thing in nature is, by creation, limited to what it is. We cannot make our own universe. But man, in contrast to the animal, can consciously act upon what is there. In having dominion over nature, man is to use it, but not as though it were nothing in itself. Since the Fall, man has used his dominion wrongly. He has set himself at the center of the universe and exploited things as though he had an autonomous right to them. Christians who have returned to a recognition of Christ's Lordship do not act as though nature were nothing in itself, nor do they exploit it. Similarly, in the home a man is to be the head, but not a tyrant making his wife a slave. He is to love his wife as Christ loved the church. There is to be order in a fallen world, but in respect and love. Fallen man has dominion over nature but uses it wrongly. The Christian, however, is called upon to exhibit his dominion, and exhibit it rightly. The industrial revolution or capitalism are not necessarily wrong; their greedy abuse of nature is wrong.

Part of the image of God in man restored in regeneration is a sense of beauty. Christians in dealing with nature use it in such a way as to recognize its value and preserve its beauty. Christians, of all people, should not be destroyers. We may cut down a tree to build a house or to make a fire to keep the family warm. But we should not cut down the tree just to cut down the tree. We should not deface things simply to deface them. Killing animals for food is one thing, but they do not exist simply as things to be slaughtered. The same is true of fish: They ought not to be caught and left to rot and stink. It is wrong to deify nature and animals; it is also wrong to disrespect what God has made. Both tendencies result for well-meaning people who lack a sound Christian view of creation.

Christian homes and churches are pilot plants where men may see not only substantial healing between men and God, and men and men, but also between men and nature. The church exhibits in its own use of land, shrubbery, trees and resources that it can overcome the alienation and rebellion sin has produced. "If things are treated only as autonomous machines in a decreated world, they are finally meaningless. But if that is so, then inevitably so am I—man—autonomous and equally meaningless. But if individually, and in the Christian community, I treat with integrity the things which God has made, and treat them this way lovingly, because they are His, things change. If I love the Lover, I love what the Lover has made. Perhaps this is the reason why so many Christians feel an unreality in their Christian lives. If I don't love what the Lover has made—in the area of man, in the area of nature—and really love it because He made it, do I really love the Lover at all?"[9]

I. Consider also any social implications involved in the instances cited in chapter four under Live Options. For a local church exhibiting concern for the poor and the racially different see David R. Mains's *Full Circle: The Creative Church for Today's Society* (Waco, Tex.: Word Books, 1971), and for a monthly report on how Christianity is working, see *The Church Around the World,* Tyndale House Publishers, Wheaton, Illinois.

III. Debated Issues and Biblical Data
A. A Christian and people who are poor

1. Keep in mind that these factors often are causes of poverty: (a) Economic: A stable income that is too low for the needs of oneself or family, or an unstable income. These may be due to conditions beyond the person's control, such as a general economic depression or exploitation by others who own the means of production. (b) Family: A mother who is widowed, divorced, abandoned or unmarried and has several children. These children grow up with no model of a male provider who cares about them. (c) Psychological: Among school children, a "failure syndrome," and among parents, a despair of ever improving their situation (quite in contrast to the student who may be poor while working his way through school but has the hope of better days ahead).[10] (d) Moral: Rebellion against opportunities to work; laziness,

indolence.

2. What should be the Christian attitude toward the indolent?

Prov. 6:6	Prov. 12:11	2 Thess. 3:6-13
Prov. 10:5	Prov. 20:13	

3. What attitudes should a Christian have toward those who are not to be blamed because they are poor, such as widows, orphans and travelers from a foreign land?

Lev. 19:15	Jas. 2:1-7	1 Jn. 3:16-17
Ps. 82:3-4		

4. How is one's attitude toward God shown in his attitude toward the poor and oppressed?

Prov. 14:31

5. How were the poor in Bible times "oppressed" or exploited?

Eccl. 4:1-3	Ezek. 22:6-12	Amos 5:12
Eccl. 5:8	Amos 2:6-7	Amos 8:4
Is. 10:1-2	Amos 4:1	Mic. 2:2

6. To what end do oppressors of the poor come? How does God judge them?

Ex. 22:21-27	Jer. 21:10-12	Mic. 2:2-6
Prov. 22:16, 22-23	Ezek. 22:6-22	Zech. 7:8-14
Eccl. 7:7	Amos 3:9-11	Mal. 3:5

7. Is there any hope for one who has taken advantage of the poor?

Is. 1:12-17	Is. 58:6-12	Jer. 7:1-7
Is. 33:14-16		

8. What can the exploited do for themselves?

Ps. 9:9-10	Ps. 119:121-128	Rom. 12:14-21
Ps. 12:5-6	Is. 19:19-22	Jas. 5:1-12

9. A Chinese in Hong Kong nearly became a communist on the strength of the following argument: "Only communism permanently helps the poor by changing the unjust conditions producing poverty. Christianity offers a gift that helps temporarily and abandons the poor to the hopelessness of unchanged and unfair circumstances." Does this

argument accurately represent the Bible's teaching? What should God's people do to liberate others from unjust oppression?

Job 29:12-17   Is. 1:16-17   Ezek. 22:29-30
Ps. 82:3-4   Jer. 21:12   Zech. 7:9-10
Prov. 31:8-9   Jer. 22:1-9

10. How might people in a land where the poor are oppressed pray for their leaders?

Ps. 72:1-14

11. What is necessary in addition to a proper attitude toward the needy?

Gal. 2:9-10   Jas. 2:15-16   1 Jn. 3:18
2 Cor. 8:14

12. What beneficent actions taken by God's people in Old and New Testament times can Christians carry out today?

Lev. 19:9-10, 15   Deut. 15:7-11   Lk. 14:12-14
Lev. 25:35-38   Mt. 11:5   Jas. 1:27
Deut. 14:28-29   Lk. 3:10-14

13. Should a church form a "social action committee" to care for people's needs?

Acts 6:1-6

14. Should God's people limit their concern for the welfare of others to members of their own group?

Lev. 19:34   Gal. 6:10   1 Thess. 3:12-13
Acts 11:27-30   Phil. 2:4   1 Thess. 5:15
Rom. 15:1

15. How does helping the needy reflect a Christian's understanding of the central fact of his faith?

2 Cor. 8:9   Phil. 2:4-8

16. What motivation should characterize Christian almsgiving?

Mt. 6:1-4   Lk. 12:32-34   2 Cor. 8:1-7
Lk. 11:37-42

17. What does giving of himself and his resources do for the sincere giver?

Ps. 41:1   Prov. 22:9   Jer. 22:16

Prov. 11:24-25   Is. 58:3-12   Acts 20:35

18. When should one share with the destitute?

Prov. 3:27-28

19. Summarize this section by answering the question, How should Christians be involved in helping the poor? Show how Christians can help either directly or indirectly to alleviate each of the four factors mentioned in A1.

B. A Christian and people of different races

1. On what basis does a Christian regard all people of all races to be derived from the same family?

Gen. 3:20   Acts 17:26   Heb. 2:11

2. Why does a Christian respect the dignity and value of each human being, however different his characteristics?

Gen. 1:26-27   Gen. 9:6   Jas. 3:9

Gen. 5:1

3. Why should a Christian strive to see that all people, however different, receive justice and love?

Lev. 19:33, 36   Prov. 21:3   Rom. 13:8-14

Deut. 10:17-19   Mic. 6:8   1 Pet. 1:17

2 Chron. 19:6-7

4. In terms of passages in questions B1 to B3, evaluate the following statements of a Christian anthropologist: (a) "Remember that one's individual worth, whether more or less than that of another, is the product of his cultural learning and his spiritual relation to God—not of his race." (b) "Equality means that all human beings are entitled to equal opportunity to develop their capacities to the fullest, not that these capacities are identical."[11]

5. Did God's choice of Israel as an instrument to bring blessing to the whole world imply the superiority of the Jewish race?

Deut. 7:7-8   Rom. 11:5-6

6. For what reason did God forbid the Jews to intermarry with the Canaanites?

Ex. 34:15-16   Josh. 23:6-13   1 Kings 11:1-8

Deut. 7:3-5   Judg. 3:6-7

7. Does the Bible teach that any race is permanently destined to slavery or to unequal opportunities for education and development as a result of the sensuality of Noah and Ham?[12]

Gen. 9:25-27 (Specifically, what was predicted as the outcome of the sin?)

Gen. 10:6, 15-20 (Who were the descendants of Ham through Canaan?)

Josh. 3:10; 1 Kings 9:20-21 (When was the prediction fulfilled?)

Deut. 8:19-20 (If the same consequence followed for Israelites who similarly sinned, could the curse have anything to do with skin pigmentation?)

8. Do allusions to the practice of slavery in the Old Testament justify disregard for the dignity of any individuals in other races?

Ex. 21:1-27   Job 31:13-15   Jer. 34:8-22
Deut. 15:12-18

On the basis of your understanding of the verses in B1 to B8, evaluate the conclusion of I. Mendelsohn on slavery in the Old Testament: "It should be stressed that slavery in biblical Palestine was of a domestic character. The slave worked shoulder to shoulder with his master in the field or at home, and hence he was treated as a member, albeit an inferior one, in the large household. . . . The prophetic literature, although recognizing the existence of economic servitude, insisted upon the humanity of the slave."[13]

9. Do the New Testament instructions to masters and slaves of the first century endorse either the institution of slavery or a practice of racial discrimination?

1 Cor. 7:20-24   1 Tim. 6:1-2   Philem. 8-20
Eph. 6:5-9   Tit. 2:9-10   1 Pet. 2:18-25
Col. 3:22-25

Evaluate the conclusion on this question to which Arthur Rupprecht came: "In short, the institution of slavery is not condemned but the abuses of it are. . . . The silence of Christ and the Apostles in regard to the institution of slavery suggests that some explanation for their silence should be sought in the nature of the slave system itself. The Biblical attitude toward the master-slave relationship is based on the principle that 'the laborer is worthy of his hire.' As has been shown, a slave received a recompense in food, clothing, shelter, and spending money. His recompensation was as much or more than that of his free-born counterpart. When he was freed, his former owner loaned or gave him the money to establish himself in business. The evidence further suggests that hundreds of thousands of slaves were freed by the Romans. Therefore, it is concluded that the silence of the New Testament on the slavery question is to be explained by the essentially worthwhile character of slavery during this period. In our thinking we have too long superimposed the viciousness, perpetual bondage and race hatred of slavery in the American South on conditions in the Roman world."[14]

10. What is the significance of the teaching and example of Jesus for race relations today?

Mt. 10:5-15	Lk. 3:6	Lk. 24:47
Mt. 20:25-28	Lk. 6:20-49	Jn. 4:3-42
Mk. 7:24-30	Lk. 10:25-37	Jn. 12:20-36
Lk. 2:32	Lk. 17:11-19	

Do you agree with William Edward Raffety: "There were slaves during NT times. The church issued no edict sweeping away this custom of the old Judaism, but the gospel of Christ with its warm, penetrating love-message mitigated the harshness of ancient times and melted the cruelty into kindness. The equality, justice and love of Christ's teachings changed the whole attitude of man to man and master to servant. This spirit of brotherhood quickened the conscience of the age, leaped the walls of Judaism, and penetrated the remotest regions. . . . Christ was a reformer, not an anarchist. His gospel was dynamic, but not dynamitic. It was leaven, electric with power, but permeated with love. Christ's life and teaching were against Judaistic slavery, Roman slavery and any form of human slavery. The love of His gospel and the light of His life were destined, in time, to make human emancipation earth-wide, and human brotherhood as universal as His own benign presence."[15]

11. Are people of all races or ethnic groups (for example, Jews and Gentiles) equally fallen from their created state and guilty before God?
Rom. 3:9-20, 23

12. How does Jesus Christ's death for sinners provide the way to unite alienated peoples?
Eph. 2:11-22　　　　Eph. 3:6　　　　Eph. 4:4-6

13. Is the same reconciling gospel the hope of all the fallen members of all the races of mankind?
Mt. 28:18-20　　　　Acts 1:8　　　　Acts 8:26-39
Lk. 24:46-48

14. How does the Holy Spirit unite all believers to the body of Christ?
1 Cor. 12:12-13

15. What types of people did the Holy Spirit incorporate into the body of Christ on the day of Pentecost?
Acts 2:9-11

16. What decisive event broke down the animosity between Jews and Samaritans?
Acts 8:4-25

17. How was Peter's prejudice against the Gentiles finally overcome?
Acts 10:28-43

18. In a Christian church should racial distinctions remain a barrier to fellowship?
Gal. 3:28　　　　Col. 3:11

19. On what basis does each member of the body of Christ have full freedom to develop his Spirit-given gifts to their fullest potential?
1 Cor. 12:14-27　　　　1 Cor. 13:1-13　　　　1 Cor. 14:37-38

20. Why are there schisms in the body of Christ?
1 Cor. 3:1-4, 18-23　　　　Gal. 2:11-21　　　　Jas. 2:8-17

21. How do Christians find the dynamic to change habits of subtle, or not-so-subtle, prejudice against people of a different racial or ethnic background?
Eph. 4:22—5:20　　　　Eph. 6:10-18

22. Summarize this section by answering the question, Does genuine Christianity, as distinct from misuses of it in support of racist dogmas, have the resources to really work in today's world?

C. A Christian and violence or war against other people

1. Is a Christian justified in taking vengeance upon one who has injured him personally?

Mt. 5:9-16, 38-48   Rom. 12:14, 17-21

2. What is the spirit of prudent people in a world torn by bitter jealousy, selfish ambition, disorder and vile practices?

Prov. 1:7-19   Rom. 15:5-6   Jas. 3:13-18
Rom. 14:17-19   2 Cor. 6:1-18

3. Did Christ permit his disciples to utilize violence against those who opposed him?[16]

Mt. 13:24-30   Lk. 9:51-55   Lk. 22:35-38, 47-53
Mt. 26:47-54

4. Does Jesus' example of cleansing the temple justify guerrilla warfare against any establishment, or was the event a sign of his unique messianic identity and authority or what?[17]

Mt. 21:10-13   Mk. 11:15-19, 28

5. Can Christ's kingdom be established by violence?

Jn. 18:36-37   Rom. 14:17-19   2 Cor. 10:3-5

6. Does violence lead to permanent peace or to more violence?[18]

Mt. 26:52   Rev. 13:10

7. What did Jesus mean when he said he came not to bring peace but a sword?

Mt. 10:34-39

8. As Christ wept over the people of Jerusalem who did not receive him, what did he pray?

Lk. 19:42-44

9. How is Christ's example with regard to responding to violence to be reflected in the lives of his followers?

1 Pet. 2:21-24

10. If every human being became a faithful follower of

Jesus as Lord would there be any war in today's world? (Review passages in questions C3 to C9.)

11. Does it follow from Jesus' example that a person who does not take vengeance into his own hands because of personal harm will do nothing while others are treated unjustly? How should a Christian's holy love manifest itself in action when loved ones are violated or defenseless people are attacked?[19]

Jn. 15:13

12. Is the state divinely instituted to exercise the kind of force Christians (as individuals or as organized bodies of believers) are forbidden to use? Although force does not attain righteousness, has it a role in the prevention and punishment of selfish evildoers?[20]

Rom. 13:1-7   Tit. 3:1   1 Pet. 2:13-17

13. What is the ultimate source of war?

Jas. 4:1-2

14. If a ruler of a nation is possessed by a lust for power and attacks another defenseless nation, can Christianity be held responsible? Once the war has begun, is it the Christian thing to let the other nation face a reign of terror and enslavement without either forceful or peaceful resistance?

Gen. 14:1—15:1

15. For what reasons did God permit wars in Old Testament times?

Deut. 7:1-5   Judg. 6:1-10   Jer. 30:15
Deut. 20:15-18   2 Chron. 15:3-6   Dan 9:8-14

16. Are similar causal factors present in today's world? Must we face up realistically to the possibilities of wars as a continued part of the present fallen world-order?

Mt. 24:6

17. Does God take any pleasure in war? What is his goal for a nation?

1 Chron. 22:8-9   Is. 65:17-25   2 Cor. 13:11
Is. 2:1-4   Ezek. 18:23-32   Heb. 13:20
Is. 9:6-7   Mt. 5:9

18. In the Old Testament context, did the command "Thou shalt not kill" forbid hunting (or sacrificing) animals, capital punishment or participation in war, or merely murder, the taking of human life in personal vengeance?

Ex. 20:13	Deut. 20:1-4	1 Sam. 7:8-11
Lev. 24:21	Josh. 11:16-23	2 Sam. 5:19, 25
Num. 35:16-34	Judg. 2:23—3:10	1 Chron. 5:22
Deut. 19:11-13		

19. Can a government be demonically misused in idolatrous and bestial ways?

Rev. 13:1-18

20. Is God able to overrule coalitions of nations that conspire against his reconciling purposes in his Son?

Ps. 2:1-11

21. What will be the purpose of the final battles on earth?

| 2 Thess. 1:5-10 | Rev. 17:14 | Rev. 19:11-21 |
| Rev. 16:14-16 | | |

22. For the present time, what can a Christian do to promote peace throughout the world?

| Mt. 5:9 | Gal. 6:10 | Heb. 12:14 |
| Gal. 5:22 | 1 Tim. 2:1-3 | |

23. Summarize this section by relating the Bible's teaching on peace (questions 1-10) to its teaching on war (questions 11-22). Then, in light of your conclusions, evaluate the attempted reconciliation of William E. Nix, and, finally, show how your view applies to the use of nuclear weapons, which no longer allow war to be the plaything of professionals but can exterminate whole societies. (It would also be instructive and interesting to apply your position to the involvement of Christians in the crusades to recover the Holy Land from the Moslems 1095-1291 and to America's Revolutionary War, Civil War and War in Vietnam.)

Nix criticizes pacifism, total disassociation from war of any kind whether as aggressor or defender, on the grounds that it (a) mistakenly applies Jesus' ethic for individuals to society as a whole, (b) fails to account for the Old Testament teaching on war and so undermines the essential continuity of biblical ethics, reflecting an apparently changing morality for God himself, (c) was inapplicable in the history of the church and (d) leads to "dropoutism" in all areas of political activity, such as the payment of taxes and citizen participation in government.

He also criticizes the "activist" position that Christians are to be involved in war whenever their country takes such a stance. This blind obedience to the state, which gave rise to the Nazi atrocities during World War II, is an overly simplistic application of the Bible's teaching that the believer should submit to the government that exists as an institution ordained of God. Not only does unquestioned loyalty to the state lead to moral bankruptcy, but no nation today can legitimately claim to be a theocratic kingdom, a chosen nation of God. Hence total submission to the state is, in actuality, a form of idolatry. One gives total allegiance to something that is less than absolute.

Nix then sketches a third, "mediativist" position. The mediativist assumes that the moral teachings of the Sermon on the Mount do not militate against "just" war and that the obligation to "obey God rather than man" (Acts 5:29) does not automatically exclude war altogether. Instead, he maintains:

> The believer is obligated to submit himself to authority until and unless that authority compels him to place that authority before God. The mediativist argues that it may be obligatory for him to support his government if the cause be truly "just" and the activities he is called upon to perform do not compel the believer to condone every individual nation within a war, even if that war be "just." . . . The mediative position is not simplistic. Instead, it is too complex to provide an easy guide for believers who want to avoid personal responsibility for their own decisions. . . . Having made a distinction in his own mind between Americanism and Christianity, and recognizing that capitalism

is a materialistic philosophy just as is communism, the mediativist is left with the problem of making moral decisions in a world filled with secular values. . . . For a believer, then, obedience to a given authority is no longer to be considered as absolute, and resistance is brought into focus as a practical and live option. Individual human acts must be scrutinized and have applied to them scriptural criteria which will guard them against subjective misjudgment. It becomes essential for individual believers to reinsert their morality into their ostensibly secular activities. . . . In such a situation the believer can no longer enjoy the protective cocoon of the pacifist position, which is too simplistic in its denial of Christian responsibility. Nor can he any longer cover his head in the sands of moral ostrichism by completely submitting himself to a less than ultimate authority in the state. Instead, he must follow in the footsteps of those who have stood fast to their moral convictions with their lives. The examples of the midwives in Egypt just prior to the Exodus, Elijah, the Hebrew children in Babylon during Daniel's time, Jeremiah (who seems to have spent more of his adult life in jail than out because of his opposition to the government), the Apostle John (who spent time in exile on Patmos), and the countless Christians who have resisted authority when it demanded allegiance before God, have earned the esteem and respect of believers throughout history.[21]

D. The Christian's use of mankind's limited "life-support system"

1. Ecology avoids the specialization of the other sciences and takes a systems approach to nature, studying living organisms and the nonliving environment together as a whole, an ecosystem. Thinking in compartments, according to a *Time* magazine essay, is the road to environment disaster. People must see the world in terms of unities rather than units and must perceive the relative value and order of each part for the whole.[22] "What is new is the melodramatic reali-

zation, just recently come over us, that ecology represents an implicative system in which man, nature, and the world are mutually interdependent for survival."[23] If Christianity has something to offer in the ecological crisis, it must provide a comprehensive system by which to determine how to make the urgent choices necessary to preserve each aspect of the life-support system of spaceship earth. Are the elements of the world—sun, plant life, plant-eating animals, flesh-eating animals, processes of decomposition and nutrition—all included in a Christian system of truth and value? Is the God of the Bible the Lord of all this?

Gen. 1:1-31   Jn. 1:1-3   Acts 17:24-25

2. In a Christian system of levels of reality, is man just another animal? Is man divine? What place has man in relation to higher and lower forms of existence?

Ps. 8:1-9

3. In view of the passages in D1 and D2, was John Locke correct in considering man "absolute lord of his own person and possessions . . . subject to nobody"?[24]

4. Does God's command to man to have dominion over the earth give man the right to exploit and misuse his environment, as if he were not under God?

Gen. 1:27-28   Ps. 29:1-11   Ps. 104:1-35

Ps. 24:1-10

5. How do you interpret the command "to be fruitful and multiply and fill the earth" in a time when the usable air, water and food is being rapidly reduced by the present exploding population on the earth?

6. Can anyone genuinely love God and his neighbor while seeking his own aggrandisement by avoidably polluting his neighbor's water and air?

Jas. 2:8-17   1 Jn. 3:17-18   1 Jn. 4:20

7. As steward of all God's earthly resources, how will man be judged?

Lk. 12:48

8. Will all men have to give an account of the value they

put upon material possessions?
Lk. 12:15-21

9. How would you apply Christ's parable of the pounds to the use of natural resources (electrical energy, for example)?
Lk. 19:11-27   Compare 1 Pet. 4:10

10. Is it possible that ecological problems are a sign of the end times?
Mt. 24:7, 22, 29

11. What is a wise attitude on the part of a steward who does not know when his master will return?
Lk. 12:32-47

12. How do the words of the prophets apply to the greedy and covetous who consume more than their share of the earth's riches today?

Prov. 15:27	Jer. 6:12-13	Ezek. 33:31
Prov. 21:26	Jer. 8:9-10	Mic. 2:1-2
Is. 5:8	Jer. 22:16-17	Hab. 2:5-9
Is. 56:9-12	Ezek. 22:12-13	

13. What qualities does the Holy Spirit develop in Christians to help them overcome temptations to be wasteful and indulgent?

1 Cor. 9:19, 24-27	Eph. 5:18	Heb. 11:25
2 Cor. 12:15	Phil. 4:5	2 Pet. 1:5-8
Gal. 5:22-23		

14. Summarize this section, indicating whether you think Christianity works ecologically. Then evaluate the following suggestions of Carl H. Reidel, Assistant Director of the Center for Environmental Studies at Williams College. He points out (a) that there is no Christian justification for the accumulation of material wealth at the expense of others, (b) that individual Christians must make a *radical* reassessment of their personal values concerning material affluence and start expressing that commitment collectively, and (c) that only a change in values that makes a significant reduction in our consumption of energy will be sufficient. Then he says,

I would offer one simple step, and this, mind you, is for

Christians. Begin to tithe. I realize that is a rather shop-worn reply, but I know of no better way to face up to the personal question of one's own attitude toward material affluence. Learning to give up a tenth of his income will tell a person more about his willingness to make sacrifices for the good of others than any academic discussion. If a really committed Christian can't share a tenth of his income for the work he claims is most important to him, I don't think I can convince him to worry about 'the ant,' or starving South Americans, or Lake Erie. Furthermore, we can link the tithe to environmental concern by making that reduction in our own consumption count environmentally: supporting those industries that are ecology-conscious, getting a smaller car, and generally consuming less. This would have a major impact nationally and make our tithe count twice—for the Lord and for the environment. A fully tithing church would also be in a position not only to launch direct environmental efforts, but also to tell a world about a life style that gets at the root of the problem. Christianity has a lot to say about the effects of materialism on man's relation to nature and to his fellow man, and how those relations can be changed by a relationship with God through Jesus Christ. Indeed, in terms of value systems, the Christian ideal holds the ultimate answer to the environmental crisis.[25]

IV. Conclusion

Formulate your answer to the question "Does a Christian's faith really work in his relationships with others?" by pulling together your summaries of the preceding sections, evaluating the live options (II) with which you differ and interacting with any reading you have done in the sources listed in the notes below.

V. Relevance

A. Make a personal inventory of the last year of your life,

listing ways in which you have matured in your relationships to the poor, the racially different, your nation's enemies and your neighbor's ecological interests.

B. Project ways in which you can improve and contribute more significantly in each of these areas in the coming year.

Notes

[1] Pierre Berton, *The Comfortable Pew* (Philadelphia: J. B. Lippincott, 1965), p. 127.

[2] Ibid., pp. 68, 37, 83.

[3] J. T. Seamands, "Frank Laubach: 'Apostle to the Illiterates,' "*World Vision Magazine,* March 1971, pp. 4-7; Frank E. Laubach, *How to Teach One and Win One for Christ* (Grand Rapids: Zondervan, 1964).

[4] David O. Moberg, *Inasmuch: Christian Social Responsibility in 20th Century America* (Grand Rapids: Wm. B. Eerdmans, 1965), pp. 62, 75, 87, 108, 118, 94; "David O. Moberg," *Social Compass,* 17 (1970/2), pp. 261-308.

[5] "Western Civilization, a Curse or a Blessing?" *The African Challenge,* No. 236 (n.d.), p. 11.

[6] Tom Skinner, *How Black Is the Gospel?* (Philadelphia: J. B. Lippincott, 1970), pp. 65-85.

[7] John B. Anderson, *Between Two Worlds: A Congressman's Choice* (Grand Rapids: Zondervan, 1970), pp. 37-38, 74, 112, 114.

[8] Jacques Ellul, *Violence: Reflections from a Christian Perspective* (New York: The Seabury Press, 1969), pp. 94-108, 129, 152-53, 164-65.

[9] Francis Schaeffer, *Pollution and the Death of Man: The Christian View of Ecology* (Wheaton, Ill.: Tyndale House, 1970), pp. 33, 54, 67-73, 91-92.

[10] Lewis B. Smedes and others, "Poverty in America," *The Reformed Journal,* January 1968, pp. 12-26; "Can Affluent America End Poverty?" *U.S. News and World Report,* August 14, 1972, pp. 23-29.

[11] J. Oliver Buswell III, *Slavery, Segregation and Scripture* (Grand Rapids: Wm. B. Eerdmans, 1956), pp. 91, 78.

[12] Merrill F. Unger, *Archaeology and the Old Testament* (Grand Rapids: Zondervan, 1954), pp. 74-77; Columbus Salley and Ronald Behm, *Your God Is Too White* (Downers Grove, Ill.: InterVarsity Press, 1970), pp. 84-87.

[13] I. Mendelsohn, "Slavery in the Old Testament," in *The Interpreter's Dictionary of the Bible* (New York: Abingdon Press, 1962), IV, p. 387.

[14] Arthur Rupprecht, "Christianity and the Slavery Question," *Bulletin of the Evangelical Theological Society,* 6, No. 2 (May 1963), p. 68.

[15] William Edward Raffety, "Slave, Slavery," *International Standard Bible Encyclopedia* (Grand Rapids: Wm. B. Eerdmans, 1949), IV, p. 2,817.

[16] Jimmy R. Allen, "The Bible Speaks on War and Peace," in *Peace! Peace!* ed. Foy Valentine (Waco, Tex.: Word Books, 1967), pp. 26-47.

[17] On recent attempts to interpret Jesus as a political revolutionary see Vernon Grounds, *Revolution and the Christian Faith* (Philadelphia: J. B. Lippincott, 1971), especially pp. 107-22.

[18] On the "laws of violence," see Jacques Ellul, *Violence: Reflections from a Christian Perspective* (New York: The Seabury Press, 1969), especially pp. 93-108.

[19] Discussion from the pacifist position and other viewpoints may be found in "War and the New Morality," *The Reformed Review,* February 1968, pp. 5-33; see also David H. Adeney, *China: Christian Students Face the Revolution* (Downers Grove, Ill.: InterVarsity Press, 1973), pp. 1-130.

[20] See Vernon Grounds, "A Just Revolution?" in *Revolution and the Christian Faith,*

pp. 125-85; and J. Oliver Buswell, Jr., "The Biblical Doctrine of the State," in *A Systematic Theology of the Christian Religion* (Grand Rapids: Zondervan, 1962), I, pp. 400-13.

[21] William E. Nix, "The Evangelical and War," *Journal of the Evangelical Theological Society*, 13, No. 3 (Summer 1970), pp. 133-46. See reading list below.

[22] "Fighting to Save the Earth from Man," *Time*, February 2, 1970, pp. 57, 63.

[23] Hugh T. Kerr, "Ecosystems and Scystematics," *Theology Today*, 29, No. 1 (April 1972), p. 133.

[24] John Locke, "An Essay Concerning the True Original Extent and End of Civil Government," in *Great Books of the Western World* (Chicago: Encyclopedia Britannica, 1937), XXXV, p. 53.

[25] Carl H. Reidel, "Christianity and the Environmental Crisis," *Christianity Today*, April 23, 1971, p. 8.

Suggested further reading on the Christian and war

Roland Bainton, *Christian Attitudes Toward War and Peace* (New York: Abingdon, 1960). A history of Christian positions on war.

Richard H. Bube, *The Human Quest: A New Look at Science and the Christian Faith* (Waco, Tex.: Word Books, 1971), pp. 238-43. "Consider the revolutionary impact of even such a minimal pledge by all Christians in the world as the following: In view of the unity of the Body of Christ, I will neither engage in nor support war or violence directed against any other Christian" (p. 243).

"Crusades," *The Westminster Dictionary of Church History* (Philadelphia: Westminster, 1971), pp. 249-51.

H. E. Guillebaud, *Some Moral Difficulties of the Bible* (London: Inter-Varsity, 1949), pp. 126-35. War is an evil, according to Scripture. God takes no pleasure in it, but permits and utilizes it as a "sore judgment" (Ezek. 14:21) for Israel when her cause is just and against her when she has fallen into the evils of the nations round about her. The Canaanites were destroyed for the same reason as those of Noah's day or of Sodom and Gomorrah, only the instrument of divine providence was different.

Peter W. Macky, *Violence: Right or Wrong?* (Waco, Tex.: Word Books, 1973), pp. 1-206. Attributes Old Testament teaching on violence and war to Israel's neighbors and emphasizes Jesus' nonviolent, peacemaker role. Summarizing his own work, Macky says: "Question: What is the chief cause of violence? Answer: Violence. Question: What is the cure for violence? Answer: Nonviolence. Question: How do people become nonviolent? Answer: By conversion."

Bernard L. Ramm, *The Right, the Good and the Happy* (Waco, Tex.: Word Books, 1971), on selective pacifism and the Nuremburg trials, pp. 138-40; on just war and atomic war, pp. 140-41.

Sherwood Wirt, *The Social Conscience of the Evangelical* (New York: Harper & Row, 1968), pp. 122-25. Defends war in order to protect freedom. "Will a man fight for his freedom? Because if he won't, in a sinful planet he will not have it long."